Ten Speed Press
P.O. Box 7123
Berkeley, CA 94707

Distributed in Australia by E.J. Dwyer Pty Ltd; in Canada by Publishers Group West; in New Zealand by Tandem Press; in South Africa by Real Books; and in the United Kingdom and Europe by Airlift Books.

Design by Sydney Butchkes
Printed in Singapore

Library of Congress Cataloging-in-Publication Data
Penza, John
Sicilian Vegetarian Cooking: 99 more recipes to love /
by John Penza; illustrated by Miriam Dougenis.
p.cm.
Includes index.
ISBN 0–89815–868–0
Vegetarian cookery.   2. Cookery, Italian—Sicilian style.
I. Title.
TX837.P46 1997
641.5'636—dc20
96–8210
CIP
1 2 3 4 5—00 99 98 97

SICILIAN VEGETARIAN Cooking

99 MORE RECIPES TO LOVE
by JOHN PENZA

illustrated by MIRIAM DOUGENIS

Ten Speed Press
Berkeley, California

Contents

Introduction / *9*

I Appetizers / **15**

  1 Marinated Mixed Vegetables / 16
  2 Eggplant, Olive, and Sundried Tomato Salad / 17
  3 Eggplant "Caviar" / 18
  4 Olive Paste / 19
  5 Sicilian Hummus / 20
  6 Sautéed Spinach / 21
  7 Lemon Broccoli / 22
  8 Steamed Artichokes / 23
  9 Marinated Mozzarella / 24
10 Roasted Pepper Salad / 25
11 Potato Croquettes / 26
12 Roasted Beets / 27
13 Baked Zucchini with Oregano / 28
14 Tomato Bruschetta / 29
15 Arugula Toast / 30
16 Broad Beans / 31
17 Baked Lima Beans / 32
18 Braised Fennel / 33

II Soups / **35**

19 Basic Vegetable Broth / 36
20 Vegetable Soup / 37
21 Lentil Soup / 38
22 Cauliflower-Tomato Soup / 39
23 Escarole Soup with Ravioli and Parmesan / 41
24 Mushroom-Polenta Soup / 42
25 White Bean Soup with Orecchiette / 43
26 Split Pea Soup with Tortellini / 44
27 Egg Soup / 45

III Pasta / 47

28 Linguine in Tomato Sauce / 48
29 Fusilli with Basil-Tomato Pesto / 49
30 Farfalle with Sundried Tomato and Olive Pesto / 50
31 Shells with Parsley Pesto / 51
32 Orecchiette with Corn / 52
33 Quick Baked Vegetable Lasagna / 54
34 Baked Lasagna Noodles with Broccoli and Three Cheeses / 56
35 Linguine with Fennel / 57
36 Tortellini with Leeks, Fennel, and Cauliflower / 58
37 Penne with White Beans and Mushrooms / 59
38 Spaghetti with Peas / 60
39 Fettucine with Arugula and Goat Cheese / 61
40 Farfalle with Rosemary and Saffron / 62
41 Penne in Hot Pink Sauce / 63
42 Spaghetti with Broccoli Pesto / 64
43 Cheese Ravioli with Olives, Tomatoes, Potatoes, and
     Almonds / 66
44 Penne with Tomato, Basil, Fried Eggplant, and Ricotta Salata / 68
45 Gnocchi / 69

IV Rice / 70

46 Rice with Fennel and Parsley / 72
47 Rice with Tomatoes, Basil, and Mozzarella / 73
48 Rice with Asparagus and Mushrooms / 74
49 Rice Pilaf with Mushrooms / 75
50 Rice Pilaf with Sundried Tomatoes and Roasted Peppers / 76
51 Rice Balls / 78
52 Rice Pie / 80

V Polenta / 83

53 Basic Polenta / 84
54 Polenta-Tomato Pie / 86
55 Baked Polenta with Mushrooms and Goat Cheese / 87
56 Polenta-Zucchini Casserole / 88
57 Grilled Polenta with White Beans and Arugula / 89
58 Fried Polenta with Sundried Tomatoes and Olives / 90
59 Creamy Polenta / 91

VI Pizzas / 93

60 Sicilian Pizza / 97
61 Thin Crust Round Pizza with Tomatoes and Basil *or* Basil Pesto and
     Zucchini / 98
62 Pizza Rolls with Spinach, Herbs, and Cheese *or* Broccoli, Tomatoes,
     and Cheese / 100

63 Covered Pizza Stuffed with Broccoli and Mushrooms / 102
64 Calzone Filled with Eggplant and Cheese *or* Roasted Peppers and
  Cheese / 104
65 Baking Soda–Crust Calzone with Olives, Tomatoes, and Four
  Cheeses / 106
66 Tomato Pizza Bread with Rosemary and Olives / 109

VII Eggs / 110

67 Parsley Frittata / 112
68 Pepper Frittata / 113
69 Broccoli Frittata / 114
70 Tomato, Basil, and Cheese Frittata / 115
71 Mayonnaise / 116
72 Sicilian Egg Salad / 117

VIII Specialties / 118

73 Stuffed Zucchini / 118
74 Eggplant Rolls / 120
75 Baked Whole Zucchini / 122
76 Stuffed Eggplant / 122
77 Eggplant Parmesan / 124
78 Mixed Fried Vegetables / 126
79 Batter-Fried Vegetables / 128
80 Baked Stuffed Mushrooms / 129
81 Grilled Vegetables / 130
82 Stuffed Peppers / 132
83 Grilled Stuffed Mushrooms / 134
84 Mixed Vegetable Stew / 135
85 Orzo-Stuffed Tomatoes / 136
86 Potato Casserole / 137
87 Cauliflower Casserole / 138
88 Sicilian Falafel / 140
89 Fried Mozzarella Sandwiches / 143

IX Salads / 144

90 Fennel, Orange, and Mozzarella Salad / 145
91 Potato–String Bean Salad / 146
92 Provolone Salad / 147
93 Cauliflower-Fennel Salad / 148
94 Sicilian Coleslaw with Orange-Rosemary Dressing / 149
95 White Bean Salad / 150
96 Pasta Salad / 152

X Desserts / 153

97 Pine Nut Cookies / 155
98 Ricotta Pie/Grain Pie / 156
99 Cannoli / 158

Introduction

My first job was as a kitchen helper in a small pizza parlor in Brooklyn called Dominic's Pizza Paradiso. It was the summer of 1964 and I was just out of tenth grade. Dominic Gabrielli, the owner and operator, was a gentle, loveable guy who had a singing voice like Tony Bennett and a healthy Sicilian distrust of authority. "Don't be a dough head, Gianni," he'd tell me. "Don't trust any idea most people can understand quickly. It's probably propaganda. Think for yourself. Real ideas come from here"—he pointed to his gut—"inside you, and they take you years to work out. In the meanwhile, live for today—a loaf of bread, a jug of wine, and the right company—that's as close to heaven as you're going to come in this world."

My nose knew the truth of this: the aroma of hot pizza was more compelling than the most pious credo. Being near the heat and the aroma of the ovens, having all the fresh crusty pizza and calzone, sausages and peppers, veal and eggplant *parmigiana*, and meatball heroes I could eat; learning the secrets of making these delights from Dominic; earning $1.75 an hour: I thought I might well have been in heaven.

A growing boy, I stuffed myself from noon to nine. I noticed, however, that Dominic ate nothing all day except for the pears and oranges that he bought from his brother-in-law, Joey the Fruit, who had the produce store across the street. I also noticed that, except when he was testing pasta for doneness, Dominic never tasted a thing he made. He seemed to contradict his own seize-the-day outlook, and I asked him about it. He said he knew when something he was preparing was good—he didn't need to taste it. I asked him if he got hungry, hardly eating all day and being around so much food. He said that sometimes he did, but that he did not like to work on a full stomach. "I take my meals seriously, Gianni," he said. "If there's a chance of having my lunch interrupted by a customer or a delivery, I'd just as soon not eat."

I came to understand that Dominic had perfect control of his appetite. At eight-thirty every night, he'd pour himself a glass of wine and go in the back to wash up. His wife Marie would come by, usually with either the Sclafanis (Sal and Tina, friends who operated the bakery around the corner), or Joey the Fruit and Dominic's sister Nicola, or Marie's sister Janet and her boyfriend (whoever he was that month). While I closed up the shop, they would all go joking and laughing to Provenzana's, the restaurant on the next block, for some serious eating.

Since time before recorded history, the Mediterranean mind has had a deep understanding of what has come to be the metaphor of communion. In the beginning was food: having food was the same as having love, energy, money, or God. More than just the symbol of divine love, food was the substance of it. Spiritual life springs from physical well-being.

The island of Sicily lies at the heart of the Mediterranean, and in many ways it is blessed as the embodiment of the region. Its location, however, has also been a curse: Sicily is strategically valuable and subject to invasion and military domination. Centuries of foreign occupation and political corruption have made Sicilians resistant to government and suspicious of outsiders. Yet, however warily, they have assimilated other traditions. In their art and architecture, as well as in their cooking, there is a mix of Greek, Arab, Spanish, and French, as well as Italian.

Through it all, Sicily's ancient agricultural traditions endured. The sea, while it was the source of fish, was also the element on which the enemy arrived. The land had no such ambivalent meaning. Its fruits, the olive and the grape, were, respectively, the symbols of peace and eternal life. During the late Greek and early Roman periods of the Mediterranean's history, about 500 BC to 100 AD, there were great feasts for the goddesses of fertility and agriculture. From Messina to Agrigento, Trapani to Syracuse, in grottoes and in temple shrines to the Greek goddess Demeter and her daughter Persephone (who later became identified with the Roman deity Ceres—from whose name we derive the word "cereal"—and her daughter Proserpina), there remains much evidence of this devotion to the symbols of the powers-that-be in the earth. Today, in the Christian era, Mary is revered as both the source of the earth's bounty and as the mother of God. Beneath their patriarchal social customs, Sicilians do more than enjoy the fat of their land: they worship it in the forms of the earth mother, celebrating *Regina Campestra*, the *Madonna del'Agro*, and *Santa Maria di Grotta* on feast days that may date back to the feasts of Isis, the ancient Egyptian goddess of fertility.

For many centuries, most Sicilians were honest peasants who worked the hard volcanic land in the hot sun and prepared their simple food simply—sizzling fresh vegetables and herbs in hot olive oil and tossing the result with pasta or eating it with bread, then washing it down with homemade wine.

At the turn of the twentieth century, egregious corruption and the crumbling of the remnants of the feudal system caused many peasants to flee Sicily. My grandparents were among those who came to America, seeking freedom and upward mobility. Their cooking still remained rooted in the old country's soil: vegetables, braised, roasted, grilled, and fried; pasta with artichokes, peas, beans, greens, zucchini, cauliflower, and broccoli; soup and bread; egg pies; and simple green salads. Meat meant poultry once or twice a week and fish on Friday. Of course, in America, where every man is king, Sunday meals tended to be Neapolitan-style— bigger than they were in the old country—involving pasta with red meat sauce followed by roast beef, veal, or pork. There was cheese, but little butter and no milk or cream. This diet was maintained pretty steadily until the fifties and sixties, when I grew up. Sicilian-American baby boomers ate more cheese, eggs, and meat. Money was loose and everyone snacked on pizza and big hero sandwiches at places like Dominic's Pizza Paradiso. Now, after four generations on American pavement, much has changed in Sicilian families. Both the simple old weekday diet and the big Sunday afternoon feasts are mostly gone, victims of life in the fast lane.

But what goes around comes around. Today, as lighter meals are sought, the old ways seem fresh. Vegetables have become the food of choice rather than of necessity. Roughly forty percent of the ingredients in this book's recipes come from grain: wheat, rice, and corn. Another forty percent are vegetables, fruits, nuts, peas, and beans. About fifteen percent are dairy products—mostly cheeses—and cooking oil. You will see little butter and no milk or cream in the ingredients. The remaining five percent are sweets.

Personally, I find vegetarian eating most agreeable for many reasons: aesthetic, health-related, economical, and ecological. In the pursuit of sense gratification, less is often more. I love grains and vegetables for the beauty of their shape, color, and aroma. I also love the long-lasting, clean-burning energy I get from good bread, rice, and pasta; and much legitimate research shows that a diet rich in complex carbohydrates, fiber, and polyunsaturated fat—comprising cereal products, vegetables, legumes, and olive oil—is the healthiest. Then, there is the cost, both for the individual and the world. Vegetarian fare is less expensive than meat: an acre of land planted in wheat, beans, or zucchini yields a hundred times the nutrients as the same acre turned to grazing for beef cattle.

Of course, this is not to say one should *never* eat meat, poultry, or fish. Rather, let it be as it was in the beginning: fish or poultry once or twice a week; red meat once or twice a month. The golden mean—moderation—that's the way: the wise man sees the whole pizza, but feels free not to eat it all. Instead, he seeks harmony between his appetite and his taste and sense of proportion.

I outlined most of the recipes for this book on a recent trip to Sicily. Going through the markets, and eating in restaurants, trattorias, and pizzerias, I collected traditional recipes and gathered ideas for original ones. I supplemented these with family favorites and dishes I've enjoyed preparing and eating over the years, always siding for natural, well-rounded, "start-from-scratch" meals that are healthy as well as hearty; that satisfy the appetite as well as the soul; that appeal to the senses; and that leave one with a feeling of fullness, life, and love.

Today, Sclafani's Bakery is still where it always has been; now it is run by Sal Junior. But everything else has changed. Dominic is retired somewhere in Florida and there is a video rental store where his Pizza Paradiso used to be. Joey's Fruits and Vegetables is now the site of Off-Track Betting. Provenzana's is a nationally known hamburger chain.

For me, the memories are vivid: of the Brooklyn-Sicilian love for life; for eating and cooking; for singing; for sharing meals with one's *compadres*, or with one's *amore*. I think of how Dominic's philosophy leavened my mind. He helped me understand that many of the problems of adolescence could be solved by common sense and patience. By the end of that August, I had eaten more than my fill of pizza and sandwiches, and was joining him for his afternoon fruit and coffee, waiting until I could relax and fix myself and a friend or two a big pasta dinner after the Paradiso closed for the day.

A Note on Tomatoes

If you can get fresh, ripe tomatoes, use them. Otherwise use canned tomatoes and drain them: buy whole peeled plum tomatoes imported from Italy.

Always peel fresh tomatoes before using them in these recipes. The quickest way to do this is to drop the tomato in boiling water for twenty seconds. Remove it from the water and slip it out of its skin.

Tomatoes, fresh or canned, should be drained of excess liquid by placing them in a colander or strainer after they are chopped. Adding a sprinkle of salt, tossing them, and letting them sit for 10 minutes will help them to drain.

Two medium-sized fresh tomatoes weigh about 1 pound (454 g) and, when chopped, are about 2 cups (473 mL). This is equivalent to about six fresh plum tomatoes, or eight to twelve from a can. As some varieties of plum tomatoes are fleshier than others and there are differences in the ratio of tomatoes to the juice they are packed in, there is considerable variation in the yield of canned tomatoes once they have been drained. Depending on the grade, a 28-ounce (793 g) can to a 35-ounce (1 kg) can will be needed to make 1 pound (454 g) of tomatoes.

13

I
Appetizers
Antipasti e Contorni

Once upon a time *antipasto* meant slices of meat and cheese, garnished with olives. Now in many Italian restaurants one is greeted by a table of vegetables prepared in a variety of ways, some served at room temperature, others hot.

Antipasto literally means "before food." This is misleading since antipasto *is* food—food meant to whet the appetite. *Contorno* means "contour" or "margin"; *contorni* are the side dishes that fill the edges of the plate.

One thing meatless meals can miss is a natural center of gravity. When you are having pork chops or roast beef it is easy to tell the main course from the starter and the side dishes. Some find vegetarian cooking more satisfying and balanced precisely because the dishes are more equal to one another. In vegetarian practice, antipasti, *contorni*, and main courses are all the same animal. Today's leftover entrées are tomorrow's antipasti and *contorni*.

Most of the dishes in this book could go into this chapter and be served in appetizer or side dish portions. A small wedge of polenta pie or frittata, or even a thin slice of pizza, can make a welcome addition to any starter plate, or can be served as a tidbit attending the main course. The opposite is also true. One can turn most of these appetizers or side dishes into a full meal by serving them in sufficient quantity, or by combining them with pasta, rice, polenta, beans, bread, or other vegetables.

Today many choose to serve the antipasto with nothing following, side dishes with nothing central making a meal in themselves. Called *tapas* in Spain and *mezze* in North Africa and the Middle East, this way of eating has been around the Mediterranean for some quite some time. Stone tablets from Crete dating back to the twelfth century BC describe feasts in which a bountiful variety of modest dishes were served and diners could sample a bit of this and a little of that.

Of course, any meal that starts off with five or six appetizers is going to be a feast, while a simple, single antipasto can make a meal of plain pasta or rice seem festive. And remember, if you have more courses coming, keep antipasto portions small. Antipasti are supposed to whet appetites, not spoil them.

1
Marinated Mixed Vegetables
Insalata Mista all'Aceta

Any kind of vegetable can go into this dish—broccoli, cauliflower, carrots, bell peppers (capsicums), asparagus, mushrooms, zucchini (courgettes), artichoke hearts, celery, or string beans—either in combination or alone. Serve vegetables by themselves or on top of fresh arugula (rocket) or lettuce. Be as creative as you like with vegetable shapes and combinations. If you are using artichokes, use only the hearts. Trim as described in the recipe for Steamed Artichokes (page 23), then cut the hearts into quarters and rub them with additional lemon juice.

Serves 6 to 8

¼ cup (59 mL) olive oil

¼ cup (59 mL) balsamic vinegar

2 tablespoons (30 mL) lemon juice

4 sprigs Italian parsley

4 fresh basil leaves

1 clove garlic

Salt to taste

½ teaspoon crushed red pepper flakes, or to taste

5 cups (907 g) broccoli, red bell pepper, cauliflower, zucchini, mushrooms, or your choice of vegetables, washed, trimmed, and chopped into bite-sized pieces

12 oil-cured black olives, pitted and halved (optional)

Place oil, vinegar, lemon juice, parsley, basil, garlic salt, and red pepper in a blender and blend until smooth.

Toss the cut vegetables with the dressing. Add the olives if using them. Cover and marinate overnight in a cool place. Serve at room temperature.

2
Eggplant, Olive, and Sundried Tomato Salad
Capunatina

Capunatina is an old standby with a thousand variations.
Here is one using sundried tomatoes. This can be served at
room temperature as an antipasto; it can also be eaten warm
with pasta. It will keep for a week or more in the refrigerator.
Use sundried tomatoes that have been packed in oil.

Makes about 4 cups (946 mL)

1½ pounds (681 g) eggplant (aubergine), peeled and cut
into ½-inch (1 cm) cubes

Coarse salt

1 clove garlic, crushed or finely chopped

¼ cup (59 mL) olive oil

¼ teaspoon crushed red pepper flakes

½ onion, chopped (about ½ cup)

2 stalks celery, chopped (about 1 cup)

8 sundried tomatoes packed in oil, chopped

2 tablespoons pine nuts

10 large green Sicilian olives, pitted and cut into slivers

2 tablespoons (30 mL) balsamic vinegar

2 tablespoons (30 mL) tomato paste

Place eggplant in a bowl, sprinkle generously with coarse salt, and let
sit for 30 minutes. Drain off excess liquid.

In a heavy pot, heat the garlic in half of the olive oil. Add the eggplant
and sauté over medium high heat for 4 minutes, stirring, until the eggplant is fairly soft and slightly browned. Remove eggplant from the pan
with a slotted spoon and set aside.

Add the remaining olive oil and the red pepper flakes and onion to the
pot. Sauté over medium heat, stirring, for 2 minutes. Add the celery and
stir for 2 more minutes. Add the sundried tomatoes, pine nuts, and olives
and stir for 2 more minutes.

Lower the heat and add the reserved eggplant, the balsamic vinegar,
and the tomato paste. Mix well, cover, and cook for 25 to 30 minutes,
stirring occasionally, until the eggplant is thoroughly soft but retains its
shape. Remove from heat and serve warm with pasta, or at room temperature by itself.

3
Eggplant "Caviar"
Pesto alla Melanzano

This is related to the Greek *melitzanosalata*. I have often heard this spread referred to as "poor man's caviar"—it is a bit of a stretch to say it tastes like caviar, but it's wonderful nonetheless.

Serve with bread, bread sticks, or raw vegetables; enjoy it as a sandwich spread with tomato and cheese, or warm it and toss with short pasta such as *farfalle* or penne. For variety, add a piece of green bell pepper (capsicum), some basil leaves, or a fresh tomato. Whereas Greeks and Syrians might add yogurt, Sicilians add a tablespoon or two of ricotta cheese. You may also substitute 2 tablespoons (30 mL) of balsamic vinegar in place of the lemon juice, if you wish.

Makes about 2 cups (473 mL)

1 pound eggplant (aubergine)

¼ cup (39 g) chopped onion (about ⅓ of an onion)

¼ cup (5 g) loosely packed chopped Italian parsley

3 tablespoons (44 mL) olive oil

¼ cup (59 mL) lemon juice

1 clove garlic

Salt to taste

Crushed red pepper flakes to taste

Preheat the oven to 400°F (200°C/gas 6).

Pierce the eggplant's skin several times, place it in a baking dish, and bake until the skin wrinkles and the pulp feels soft, about 40 minutes.

Let the eggplant cool briefly, then cut it in half and scoop out the pulp. Let drain in a colander for 10 minutes.

Place the eggplant with all the other ingredients in a blender and blend until smooth. Chill for an hour or more before serving; it is really best the second day.

4
Olive Paste
Pesto al' Olivi

Olive paste can be spread on pieces of toast or served with slices of raw vegetables as an antipasto, or used as sauce for pasta. Similar dishes are made with black olives in Greece, and with niçoise olives in France. Sicilians favor their native large green olives, which are available in this country at Italian groceries and gourmet shops. For a truly Sicilian flavor, add the liqueur amaro in place of the rum. This recipe will yield enough to dress 1 pound (454 g) of pasta. Because of its strong, hot flavor, a little bit goes a long way.

Makes about 1 cup (237 mL)

4 ounces (113 g) large green Sicilian olives, pitted
1 clove garlic
1 sprig Italian parsley
1 teaspoon capers
¼ teaspoon thyme
1 teaspoon rosemary
1 tablespoon (15 mL) lemon juice
2 tablespoons (30 mL) olive oil
¼ teaspoon crushed red pepper flakes
1 tablespoon (15 mL) rum or amaro liqueur

Place all ingredients in a blender or food processor and blend until you have a paste. Use immediately or store in a sealed container in the refrigerator for up to two weeks.

5
Sicilian Hummus
Pesto al' Fagioli

This savory, easy-to-make, high-fiber spread goes with any
kind of bread, toasted or plain; crackers; strips of raw bell
pepper (capsicum); carrots; or celery sticks. It can also be
tossed with pasta or with cooked vegetables such as broccoli
or zucchini (courgettes). Cashews or walnuts can be
substituted for the pine nuts.

Makes about 2 cups (473 mL)

¾ cup (149 g) dried chickpeas, or 1½ cups (276 g) canned
¼ cup (46 g) pine nuts
⅓ cup (78 mL) lemon juice
8 fresh basil leaves
¼ cup (14 g) packed chopped Italian parsley leaves
½ teaspoons cumin powder
1 clove garlic
¼ cup (59 mL) olive oil
Salt to taste

If using dried chickpeas, soak overnight in 3 cups (710 mL) of water.
Alternatively, you may bring 4 cups (946 mL) of unsalted water to a boil
in a heavy pot. Add the dried chickpeas and boil for 5 minutes. Remove
from heat and let sit, covered, for 2 hours, then boil for 45 minutes. Add
salt only after cooking. Drain the chickpeas. Place all ingredients in a
blender or food processor and blend until smooth. Serve, or store in an air-
tight container in the refrigerator for up to 7 to 10 days.

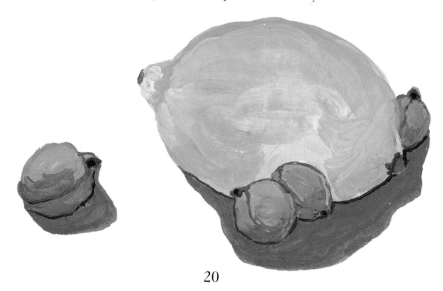

6
Sautéed Spinach
Spinaci Stufato

This recipe can be used for any greens: broccoli rabe (rapini),
escarole, arugula (rocket), or beet greens. All must have their
hard stems trimmed off and be washed well in cold water,
dried, and chopped. The method of cooking, *stufato*, calls for
olive oil to be heated in a pot on a hot range, usually with
crushed red pepper, sometimes with garlic. The greens are
then tossed in, quickly stir-fried until they are wilted, and
then cooked until tender. For variety, try adding a pinch of
nutmeg or a squeeze of lemon juice. The greens can be
served warm or at room temperature. They can also be
tossed with pasta. Spinach prepared this way makes an
outstanding filling for sandwiches.

Serves 4 to 6

10 ounces (283 g) spinach
¼ teaspoon crushed red pepper flakes
Chopped garlic to taste (optional)
3 tablespoons (44 mL) olive oil
Salt to taste

Remove coarse stems from the spinach. Wash and dry the leaves thoroughly, and chop them coarsely. Heat the red pepper flakes (and garlic if
you are using it) in the oil. When it is very hot, add the spinach, stirring
continuously until it is evenly wilted. Lower the heat, add salt, cover,
and cook until tender.

7
Lemon Broccoli
Broccoli al'Limone

This recipe will also work for cauliflower, although
cauliflower has a slightly longer cooking time.

Serves 6 to 8

1 head broccoli
Salt
Juice of 1 lemon
2 tablespoons (30 mL) olive oil

Thoroughly wash the broccoli in cold water. Remove the lower part of
the broccoli stalk and discard. Place the whole head into a large pot of
cold, salted water. Cover, place on the range, and bring to a boil over
high heat. For al dente broccoli, remove pot from heat immediately when
the water boils. If you like it more tender let it boil slowly for a minute
or two. Drain. If you like, reserve the cooking water for soup stock.

When the broccoli is cool enough to handle, cut the florets from the
main stem into bite-sized pieces. Use a paring knife to cut into the broccoli stem anywhere along its edge, then take the broccoli skin between
the blade and your thumb and pull. Chop the skinned stem into small
pieces.

Place the broccoli in a serving bowl and toss with the lemon juice,
olive oil, and more salt, if you wish. Serve at room temperature.

8
Steamed Artichokes
Carciofi

In Sicily artichokes are called *cacuoccili*. They are generally smaller than their American cousins and have no chokes: baby artichokes available in North America usually have some spine in the center. The whole artichoke can be served, or only the heart. In either case, use one large artichoke per person, or several small ones, depending on their size. When preparing artichokes, rub your hands and cutting tools with lemon to prevent discoloration.

Serves 4

4 large whole artichokes (or 8 medium or 12 small)
2 lemons
Salt
Extra virgin olive oil
¼ cup (59 mL) wine vinegar (optional)

To prepare whole artichokes, slice away the stalk and the top third of the artichoke. Snap off the outer leaves until you come to leaves that are paler green and more tender. Trim any spiky points from the leaves using a sharp knife or scissors. Hold the artichoke in both hands and, using your thumbs, spread its leaves open from the top. Remove the purple leaves at the heart and scoop out the choke using a grapefruit spoon or sharp paring knife. Place the artichokes in water for 5 minutes with the juice of 1 lemon and a lemon wedge or two to prevent discoloration.

Put the artichokes in a steamer, base downward. Steam over water that has the juice and zest of 1 lemon added or you can use the soaking mixture: 20 minutes for large artichokes, 10 or 15 minutes for smaller ones.

Sprinkle with salt and additional lemon juice and serve with good olive oil for dipping.

To prepare artichoke hearts, slice away the stalk and more of the top than you would for whole artichokes—about the top half. Cut off all the leaves until you come to the tender ones nearest the heart. Cut the heart lengthwise into four sections and cut away the choke from each section. Steam the wedges over water with a little lemon juice for 5 to 10 minutes, depending on their size. Toss with more lemon juice, salt, and olive oil and serve, or marinate in a mixture of the wine vinegar, 2 tablespoons (30 mL) of olive oil, and salt for several hours or overnight. Drain marinade, and serve.

9
Marinated Mozzarella
Mozzarella al'Olio

A vegetarian antipasto would not be complete without mozzarella. Cheese balls called *bocconcini*, which are available in some supermarkets, are generally used for this, but slices of mozzarella are fine. Of course, fresh mozzarella is best.
Marinated mozzarella can be added to salads, and is especially good with Roasted Pepper Salad or in a sandwich with fresh basil and tomatoes.

Serves 4

8 ounces (227 g) mozzarella
3 tablespoons (44 mL) olive oil
½ teaspoon dried oregano
2 tablespoons finely chopped Italian parsley
½ teaspoon crushed red pepper flakes
2 tablespoons diced roasted pimiento or red bell pepper (capsicum) (see page 25)

Unless you are using little balls of cheese, cut mozzarella into ¼-inch (.6 cm)-thick slices. Combine with other ingredients in a bowl, cover, and refrigerate overnight. Allow to reach room temperature before serving.

10
Roasted Pepper Salad
Pipi Sott'Olio

This salad is good tossed with pasta and served hot. It also makes a good topping or filling for pizza or sandwiches. To make this recipe colorful as well as delicious, choose bell peppers (capsicums) of different colors: red, green, yellow, or orange. Red peppers tend to maintain their structure best after roasting.

2 pounds (907 g) assorted bell peppers (capsicums)
3 tablespoons (44 mL) olive oil
Salt to taste
½ teaspoon oregano

Preheat the broiler. Cut the peppers into quarters lengthwise and discard the seeds and ribs. Arrange the slices skin-side up in a roasting pan and place on the top rack of the oven as close to the heat as you can get it. Check the peppers often. When the skins char thoroughly, usually within 5 minutes, remove the pan from the oven. Let the peppers cool and remove their blackened skins. Toss with olive oil, salt, and oregano, and serve.

11
Potato Croquettes
Crocchetti di Patati

Lovers of garlicky mashed potatoes may add garlic according to their taste. As for most fried foods in this book, I recommend using olive oil mixed with some lighter vegetable oil, such as corn or soybean oil. The food has a lighter taste, and the mixture is more economical. Of course, if you enjoy fried foods regularly, cooking oil can be strained, refrigerated, and used for deep-frying another day.

Makes 8 croquettes; serves 4 as an appetizer or starter

1 pound (454 g) potatoes, peeled and cut into quarters
Salt to taste
2 eggs
¼ cup (5 g) loosely packed chopped Italian parsley leaves
Pressed garlic to taste (optional)
½ cup (85 g) grated Parmesan, locatelli, or pecorino cheese
¼ cup (21 g) grated mozzarella
½ teaspoon crushed red pepper flakes, or to taste
½ cup (92 g) unbleached wheat flour or semolina flour
1 cup (128 g) unseasoned dried bread crumbs (see page 28)
Olive oil and vegetable oil for deep-frying

Boil the potatoes in plenty of salted water for about 10 minutes, until cooked but not mushy. Drain in a colander, transfer to a large bowl, and mash coarsely with a fork or masher. Allow potatoes to cool. Beat one egg and add it to the potatoes along with the parsley, garlic (if using), Parmesan, mozzarella, and red pepper flakes, Mix well. Form a loaf and cut into 8 even pieces.

Spread the flour on a plate or sheet of waxed (greaseproof) paper. Dust your hands with additional flour and shape each eighth of the potato mixture into a cylindrical roll about 4 inches (10 cm) long and ½ inch (1.5 cm) in diameter. Roll them in flour to coat them evenly.

Beat the remaining egg in a bowl and spread the bread crumbs on another sheet of waxed paper. Dip the croquettes into the beaten egg, then coat them with bread crumbs.

In a heavy skillet, pour half olive oil and half vegetable oil to a depth of ¼ inch (.6 cm). Heat the oil until it is quite hot but not burning. Fry the croquettes in batches, turning to make sure they are brown on all sides. Drain on paper towels or brown paper, and keep warm in the oven.

12
Roasted Beets
Barbabietoli al Forno

Beets are high in iron and low in calories and, roasted, they are delicious either hot or at room temperature. If you have the whole beet, sauté the greens as you would spinach (see page 21) and serve the roasted beet slices on top of them.

> 2 pounds (907 g) beets (about 4 medium beets)
> 3 tablespoons (44 mL) olive oil
> Juice of 1 lemon, plus additional lemon juice (optional)
> 2 tablespoons fresh thyme, or 1 tablespoon dried
> Salt to taste
> ¼ teaspoon crushed red pepper flakes, or to taste
> Dry white wine (optional)

Preheat the oven to 350°F (180°C/gas 4).

Trim the tops and roots from the beets and wash the beets well. It is not necessary to peel them. Cut beets into ¾-inch (2 cm) slices (about 3 slices per medium beet). Toss with the oil, juice of one lemon, and thyme, and season with salt and red pepper flakes. Place in a baking pan and bake uncovered for 45 minutes, checking the liquid occasionally. If the pan seems too dry, add a squeeze of lemon juice or a splash of dry white wine.

13
Baked Zucchini with Oregano
Zucchini Oreganata

This dish can be prepared with eggplant (aubergines) instead
of zucchini (courgettes). However, you must first salt the
eggplant slices and let them sit draining for ½ hour before
topping and baking. It's a sin to throw away stale bread and
buy packaged bread crumbs. To make your own, let any
good bread dry out in a paper bag in the refrigerator or other
cool dry place. When the bread is thoroughly hard, use a
hand grater, blender, or food processor to crumble it. Store
crumbs in your refrigerator in a tightly closed container.

Serves 6 to 8

1 cup (128 g) unseasoned dried bread crumbs (see above)
¼ cup (59 mL) olive oil
¼ cup (59 mL) freshly squeezed lemon juice
2 tablespoons dried oregano
1 clove garlic, pressed or minced
¼ teaspoons crushed red pepper flakes
½ cup (55 g) grated Parmesan, locatelli, or pecorino cheese
Salt to taste
4 medium zucchini (courgettes) (about 2 pounds/907 g)

Preheat the oven to 350°F (180°C/gas 4).

In a large bowl, combine bread crumbs, olive oil, lemon juice, oregano, garlic, red pepper, Parmesan, and salt. Set aside.

Wash the zucchini and trim the ends. Do not peel. Cut each zucchini into four lengthwise slices. They could be about ¼ to ½ inch (.6 to 1 cm) thick.

Place the zucchini slices on an oiled baking sheet, turning so both sides are moistened with olive oil. Arrange close together, edge to edge, and spread the bread crumb topping over them. Bake for 25 minutes, until the bread crumbs are browned and the zucchini is cooked through. For a browner top, place briefly under the broiler.

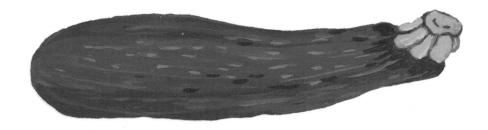

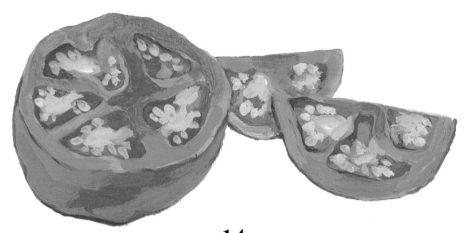

14
Tomato Bruschetta
Bruschetta al Pomodoro

Originally, *bruschetta*, or toasted bread, was used to soak up the first pressing of olive oil. Over the years the tendency to make a good thing even better resulted in the addition of garlic and eventually all sorts of other ingredients. To make a good light meal of tomato *bruschetta*, take a loaf of bread and slice it in half lengthwise, then cut it into large pieces before toasting, topping, and broiling. Known as *crostini*, such open-faced sandwiches are good topped with combinations of oil with cheese, herbs, or any "soft" vegetables you can think of. Try goat cheese and rosemary, Sicilian Hummus (page 20), or Basil-Tomato Pesto (page 49). Use good crusty Italian bread and the finest virgin olive oil.

Serves 4

¾ pound (340 g) ripe tomatoes

2 cloves garlic, pressed

Salt to taste

¼ teaspoon crushed red pepper flakes, or to taste

2 tablespoons (30 mL) olive oil

8 slices bread, ½ inch (1 cm) thick

Preheat the broiler.

Drop the tomatoes into boiling water for 20 seconds, drain, remove their skins, and chop them into small pieces. Add the garlic, salt, red pepper flakes, and olive oil. Mix well.

Toast the bread slices lightly on both sides. Spoon the tomato mixture onto the bread slices and place under the broiler for 1 to 2 minutes. Remove and serve while still warm.

15
Arugula Toast
Bruschetta con Rucola

Bunches of arugula (rocket) vary in size. The average bunch
of arugula will yield enough topping for eight slices of
baguette (fresh bread stick) or Italian bread. If you are using
bread with larger slices you will probably need more greens.
For a less sharp *bruschetta*, substitute mozzarella in place of
Parmesan.

Serves 4

1 bunch arugula (rocket), stems trimmed
2 tablespoons (30 mL) olive oil
2 cloves garlic, pressed or minced
¼ teaspoon crushed red pepper flakes
8 slices bread, ½-inch (1 cm) thick
¼ cup (43 g) coarsely grated Parmesan
Dried oregano or chopped fresh oregano
½ lemon

Preheat the broiler.

Wash, dry, and chop the leaves into small pieces. Heat the olive oil in
a skillet over medium-high heat and add the garlic and red pepper flakes.
When they start to sizzle, add the chopped arugula and stir until wilted
and reduced in size, about a minute or so. Remove from heat.

Toast the bread, lightly browning it on both sides. Divide the arugula
evenly over the toast. Put some Parmesan on each piece, then season
with a pinch of oregano and a squirt of lemon juice. Place under the
broiler until cheese melts, about a minute or two. Remove and serve.

16
Broad Beans
Fave

This dish may be served warm or refrigerated for later use as part of an antipasto plate. You can also reduce the lemon juice and add a little cooked tomato and you will have a delicious sauce to serve with pasta. Two pounds (907 g) of fresh fava (broad) beans in their pods will yield about 2 cups (340 g) of beans.

Serves 4

2 pounds (907 g) fresh fava (broad) beans, shelled
2 tablespoons (30 mL) olive oil
1 clove garlic, minced
¼ cup (59 mL) lemon juice
Salt to taste
¼ teaspoon crushed red pepper flakes, or to taste
2 tablespoons finely chopped Italian parsley

Cover the beans with cold water and bring to a boil. Remove from the heat immediately, and rinse in cold water to stop the cooking. When the beans are cool enough to handle, remove their tough outer coverings. They should slip off easily. Place the beans in a bowl and toss thoroughly with the remaining ingredients.

17
Baked Lima Beans
Fagiolini al'Forno

Use fresh beans if possible. If using frozen beans, allow them
to thaw to room temperature. A pound of fresh beans will go
a long way as an appetizer unless your family and friends are
hard-core bean lovers. This is probably better suited to be a
side dish. A casserole or other pan, such as a cast-iron skillet,
that can be used on the stove as well as in the oven is best.
For this, no lid is required.

Serves 6 to 8

1 onion, chopped

2 cloves garlic, pressed or minced

3 tablespoons (44 mL) olive oil

1 pound (454 g) lima beans

1 pound (454 g) peeled tomatoes (see page 13)

2 teaspoons dried oregano

Salt to taste

¼ teaspoon crushed red pepper flakes, or to taste

1 cup (237 mL) unseasoned dried bread crumbs (see
   page 28)

¼ cup (43 g) grated Parmesan, locatelli, or pecorino cheese

2 tablespoons (30 mL) lemon juice

Preheat the oven to 350°F (180°C/gas 4).

Sauté onion and garlic in 2 tablespoons (30 mL) of olive oil until soft,
about 5 minutes. Remove from the heat. Mix in the beans, tomatoes,
oregano, salt, and red pepper flakes. Set aside.

Mix the bread crumbs with the Parmesan, lemon juice, and the remaining olive oil. Spread this on top of the beans and bake for 30 minutes. Serve as a side dish.

18
Braised Fennel
Finocchio

Raw fennel wedges are put on the table during a big meal as
a snack between courses, to help digestion. Cooked fennel is
less common but no less delicious, and makes a fine starter.
Ideally, use a pot or casserole with a lid that is at home on the
range or in the oven.

> **2 fennel bulbs**
> **3 tablespoons (44 mL) olive oil**
> **3 tablespoons (44 mL) dry white wine**
> **Salt to taste**

Remove the tops and the outer layers from the fennel. Finely chop a
few of the leaves and reserve them. Discard other leaves and trimming.
Cut the bulbs lengthwise into ¼-inch (.6 cm) slices. Remove some of the
base, leaving enough so that the slices remain intact.

Preheat the oven to 350°F (180°C/gas 4).

In the pot or casserole, heat the olive oil over medium heat. Add the
fennel and sauté lightly for about 3 minutes, making sure the oil thoroughly coats the fennel pieces. Add the wine and salt. Cover, place in
the oven, and bake for 30 minutes.

Garnish with the reserved chopped fennel leaves and serve hot from
the oven.

II
Soups
Zuppe

Soup, like antipasto, is a way to begin a meal. Italian vegetable soup is thick and sensual. Hearty soups, most of them containing pasta, also make satisfying main courses if served with good bread and virgin olive oil or goat cheese.

Good soup starts with a good base. You can make one from scratch using the recipe below or, if you are short on time, use either tomato juice (especially that drained from canned imported plum tomatoes) or vegetable juice diluted with water. You can use water from cooking beans or vegetables. There are vegetable bouillon cubes on the market, but read the labels; most of them contain little but monosodium glutamate, garlic salt, and artificial flavor. If you don't care about being a *paisano*, you can also give soup a stock flavor by using 1 tablespoon (15 mL) of soy sauce per 2 cups (473 mL) of water. Or you can even use plain water, adding some additional vegetables or beans to the soup.

"Soup" pastas include *pennete, conchigliette, tubette, ditalini, riso, orzo,* elbows, *acini,* or any large pasta broken into smaller pieces.

Unless otherwise noted, the following recipes will yield between two and three quarts (about two to three liters) of soup, which is a starter course for six to eight people, or a main course for four. A large, heavy stockpot made of stainless steel or enameled cast iron is essential for soup making.

19
Basic Vegetable Broth
Brodo

As well as being a base for other soups and dishes such as risotto and polenta, this clear soup made of vegetable stock can be enjoyed alone, with pasta. For a light pasta soup first course, you can use any macaroni, small or large. I enjoy eating it with a twirl of vermicelli. In any case, cook the pasta in the broth just before serving. Broth can be stored in the refrigerator for several days or in the freezer indefinitely. The vegetables listed below are suggestions for a basic flavor; you can use any scraps or leftovers you have. You may wish to experiment with other stocks by adding garlic, turnips, parsnips, lentils, beans, basil, thyme, sage—or even, for a real down-home Sicilian flavor, fennel bulb or leaves.

Makes 3 quarts (2.8 L)

2 onions, chopped
1 bunch scallions (spring onions), trimmed and chopped
4 carrots, peeled and chopped
4 stalks celery, chopped
1 pound (454 g) tomatoes (see note on page 13)
1 bunch Italian parsley, washed and chopped
½ cup (100 g) dried chickpeas
1 tablespoon salt
1 tablespoon whole black peppercorns
3 quarts (2.8 L) cold water

Place all ingredients in a large pot and bring to a boil. Lower heat, cover, and simmer, for an hour or two. Then strain. After straining, you may purée the boiled vegetables and use them to thicken your soup, if you wish. Serve, use, or store.

20
Vegetable Soup
Minestrone

You can improvise with this recipe by using almost any
vegetable, legume, or pasta. Another interesting variation is
to make a rice soup by adding 1 cup (227 g) of Arborio rice 20
minutes before the end of cooking. You can cut kitchen time
significantly if you use canned beans. If you have extra water
from preparing dried beans, by all means add it to the soup.

Serves 6

½ cup (85 g) canned chickpeas, or ¼ cup (50 g) dried
1 cup (170 g) canned cannellini beans, or ½ cup (85 g) dried
½ cup (100 g) split peas
2 tablespoons (30 mL) olive oil
¼ teaspoon crushed red pepper flakes, or to taste
2 cloves garlic, minced or crushed
1 onion, chopped
2 carrots, peeled and cut into ½-inch (1 cm) rounds
1 potato, cut into ½-inch (1 cm) dice
1 cup (85 g) washed, stemmed, and chopped spinach
1 cup (85 g) julienned savoy cabbage
6 cups (1.4 L) Vegetable Broth (page 36)
1 teaspoon dried thyme
½ teaspoon dried oregano
1 cup (398 g) peeled, chopped tomatoes (see page 13)
20 whole basil leaves
¼ cup (5 g) loosely packed Italian parsley leaves
Salt and black pepper to taste
1 cup (113 g) orzo or other small pasta
Grated Parmesan for the table

To prepare beans, soak dried chickpeas and cannellini beans overnight, and boil for 1 hour. Soak the split peas for 1 hour before using.

In a large pot, heat the oil with the crushed red pepper and garlic. Add
the onion and sauté over medium heat for 3 minutes. Add the carrots,
potato, spinach, and cabbage. Slowly stir for another 3 to 5 minutes.

Add the broth, split peas, chickpeas, cannellini beans, thyme, oregano, tomatoes, basil, parsley, and salt and black pepper. Bring to a boil,
lower the heat, and cook 30 minutes.

Raise the heat to medium. Add the orzo and boil lightly, uncovered,
until the orzo is cooked and the soup thickens, about 7 minutes. Serve
with grated Parmesan cheese.

21
Lentil Soup
Minestra di Lenticchie

Normally, lentil soup is made with Italian bacon or sausage
meat. In this version the meaty flavor comes from the porcini
mushrooms (ceps). As the lentils are also hearty, the soup
does not suffer from lack of meat. Its thickness depends on
how long you simmer it. Make it thick in the winter and less
so in the summer.

Serves 6

1 cup (198 g) dried lentils
½ ounce (7 g) dried porcini mushrooms (ceps)
2 tablespoons (30 mL) olive oil
2 cloves garlic, pressed or finely minced
¼ teaspoon crushed red pepper flakes, or to taste
1 onion, chopped small
2 stalks celery, chopped small
2 carrots, peeled and chopped small
1 large fresh tomato, peeled and chopped (see page 13)
3 cups (710 mL) Vegetable Broth (see page 36)
½ cup (118 mL) dry red wine
½ cup (10 g) loosely packed finely chopped Italian parsley
Salt to taste
1 cup (113 g) *ditalini* or *tubetti* or other small pasta

Wash the lentils and soak them in 2 cups (473 mL) of water for 1 hour.
Soak the mushrooms separately in 1 cup (237 mL) of water for 1 hour.

Heat the olive oil in a large heavy pot. Add the garlic, the crushed red
pepper, and the onion and sauté over medium heat until the onion is
transparent, about 5 minutes. Add the celery and the carrots and continue sautéing for about 3 minutes. Drain the lentils and the mushrooms,
saving the water. Mince the mushrooms. Sauté the lentils and mushrooms briefly in the pot with the other ingredients. Add the tomato.
Then add the soaking water, broth, wine, parsley, and salt. Bring to a
boil, lower the heat, and simmer, covered, for about 45 minutes, until
the lentils are cooked. Uncover and raise the heat to medium. Add the
pasta and cook another 5 minutes, until the pasta is cooked and the
soup thickens.

22
Cauliflower-Tomato Soup
Zuppa di Cavolfiore e Pomodoro

This is a hearty autumn soup that is best made with fresh rosemary. If fresh tomatoes are not available, used canned tomatoes with their juice.

Serves 6

3 tablespoons (44 mL) olive oil

1 large onion, finely chopped

1 clove garlic, minced or pressed

¼ teaspoon crushed red pepper flakes, or to taste

1 cauliflower, cut into ½ inch (1 cm) florets

2 pounds (907 g) tomatoes, peeled and chopped (see page 13)

3 cups (710 mL) tomato juice diluted with 2 cups (473 mL) water or Vegetable Broth (page 26)

¼ cup (59 mL) dry red wine

1 tablespoon finely chopped fresh rosemary, or 1 teaspoon dried

¼ cup (44 g) polenta

¼ cup (5 g) loosely packed chopped Italian parsley leaves

Heat the olive oil with the onion, garlic, and crushed red pepper over medium heat for about 5 minutes, until the onion is clear and soft. Add the cauliflower and sauté another 2 minutes. Add the tomatoes, tomato juice and water or broth, wine, rosemary, and polenta. Bring to a boil, stirring constantly, then cover and slowly simmer for ½ hour until the cauliflower is soft. Stir in the parsley and serve hot.

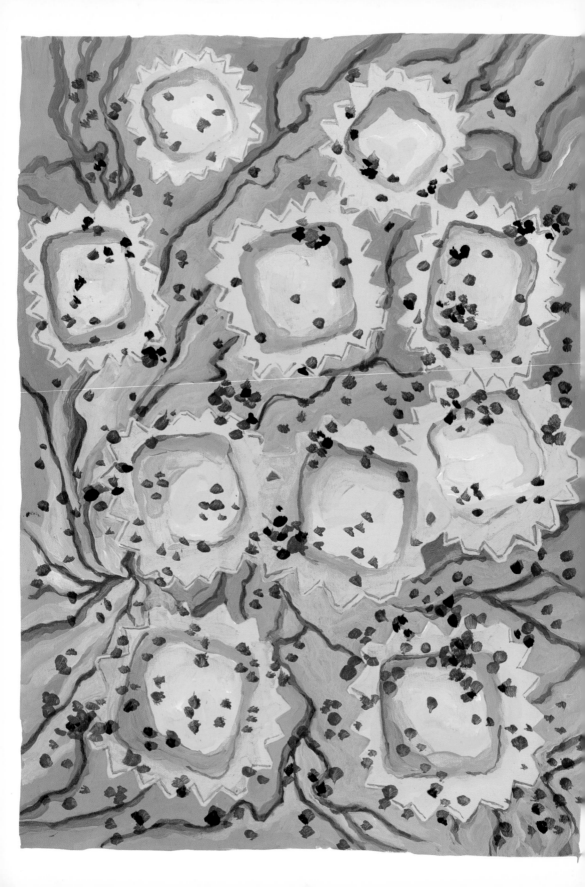

23
Escarole Soup with Ravioli and Parmesan
Zuppa di Escarole con Ravioli e Parmigiana

Escarole soup is a perennial standby. Usually it is made with chicken soup or pancetta. This variation uses vegetable broth and cheese. Keep frozen ravioli frozen until you use them. Use large ravioli for a main course, small ones for starters.

Serves 6

¼ teaspoon crushed red pepper flakes, or to taste
2 cloves garlic, pressed or minced
2 tablespoons (30 mL) olive oil
1 head of escarole, washed and chopped
6 cups (1.4 mL) Vegetable Broth (page 26)
Salt to taste
12 cheese ravioli
Coarsely grated or finely diced Parmesan for the table

In a large pot, heat the crushed red pepper and the garlic in the oil over high heat. When the oil is hot but not burning add the escarole and stir quickly to reduce. Add the vegetable broth and salt. Bring to a boil, cover, reduce the heat, and simmer for 30 minutes over low heat.

Turn the heat to medium and add the ravioli, stirring occasionally to see that they do not stick to the bottom. When they rise to the top, simmer a few more moments, and serve hot with grated or diced Parmesan at the table.

24
Mushroom-Polenta Soup
Zuppa di Funghi e Polenta

This soup can have many characters. For a thicker, creamier soup, add more polenta. For a milder flavor, use ordinary mushrooms. For a stronger, meatier mushroom flavor, add ½ ounce (14 g) of dried porcini mushrooms. *Ricotta salata* is salted ricotta, a crumbly cheese available in Italian stores and at good delicatessen counters. If you cannot find it, substitute feta rather than fresh ricotta. *Ricotta salata* is salty—take this into consideration when you salt the soup.

Serves 6

1 pound (454 g) portabello mushrooms
3 tablespoons (44 mL) olive oil
1 clove garlic, pressed or minced
¼ teaspoon crushed red pepper flakes, or to taste
6 cups (1.4 L) Vegetable Broth (see page 26)
¼ cup (44 g) polenta
¼ teaspoon dried rosemary
Salt to taste
2 tablespoons finely chopped Italian parsley
4 ounces (113 g) *ricotta salata,* grated or finely crumbled

Wash the mushrooms and cut them into pieces 1 inch (2.5 cm) long and ½ inch (1 cm) wide.

Heat the olive oil in a heavy soup pot over medium heat. Add the garlic, crushed red pepper, and mushrooms. Stir gently until the mushrooms are coated with oil and soft, about 4 minutes.

Add the broth, polenta, rosemary, and salt. Raise the heat, stirring so the polenta will not lump together, until the soup starts to boil. Cover, turn the heat to low, and cook slowly for 25 minutes. Check occasionally.

Stir in the chopped parsley and cheese and serve.

25
White Bean Soup with Orecchiette
Zuppa di Pasta e Fagioli

Orecchiette are ear-shaped pasta available in Italian stores. They are best for this dish, but any smaller, shaped pasta, like *conchiglie* (small shells) will do. Use cannellini or navy beans. A 19 ounce (538 g) can, drained, will yield about 2 cups (340 g) of beans. If you are using dried beans, soak 1 cup (198 g) overnight, then boil in 4 cups (946 mL) of water until tender—about 1 hour—before using.

Serves 6

2 cloves garlic, crushed or minced

¼ teaspoon crushed red pepper flakes, or to taste

2 tablespoons (30 mL) olive oil

1 large onion, minced

2 carrots, peeled and cut into thin rounds

2 stalks celery, sliced thin

1 bunch arugula (rocket), washed, stems removed, and chopped

6 cups (1.4 mL) Vegetable Broth (page 26)

2 cups (340 g) cooked white beans

½ teaspoon dried thyme

½ teaspoon dried sage

2 bay leaves

Salt to taste

2 cups (227 g) *orecchiette*

Grated Parmesan, pecorino, or locatelli cheese for the table

Briefly heat the garlic and the crushed red pepper in the olive oil over medium heat. Add the onion and continue sautéing for 5 minutes. Add the carrots and the celery and sauté for another 2 minutes. Add the arugula and sauté for 1 minute. Add the broth, beans, thyme, sage, bay leaves, and salt. Bring to a boil, cover, lower heat, and simmer for 20 minutes. Raise the heat and add the pasta. Boil for an additional 6 to 10 minutes, uncovered, until the pasta is cooked and the soup thickens. Serve with grated cheese.

26
Split Pea Soup with Tortellini
Zuppa di Piselli e Tortellini

I learned this soup from my grandmother, who chopped the
vegetables very fine, let the split peas boil until they were
thoroughly soft, and left it at that. There was texture in her
pea soup: I have never acquired a taste for the smooth,
puréed American pea soup.

Serves 6

1 cup (198 g) dried split green peas
2 tablespoons (30 mL) olive oil
¼ teaspoon crushed red pepper flakes, or to taste
1 large onion, minced
2 carrots, peeled and shaved thin
2 stalks celery, finely diced
½ red bell pepper (capsicum), finely diced
3 cups (710 mL) Vegetable Broth (page 26)
¼ cup (5 g) loosely packed chopped Italian parsley
Salt
2 bay leaves
½ teaspoon oregano
1 pound (454 g) frozen cheese tortellini
Grated Parmesan for the table

Wash the split peas and soak them for one hour in 3 cups (710 mL)
of water.

Heat the olive oil in a heavy soup pot. Add the crushed red pepper
and the onion and sauté over medium heat for 5 minutes. Add the carrots,
celery, and bell pepper and sauté for another 2 minutes. Add the soaked
split peas and their water and stir. Add the vegetable broth, parsley, salt,
bay leaves, and oregano. Bring to a boil, then cover and lower the heat.
Simmer for 30 minutes.

Raise the heat to medium-high, uncover, add the frozen tortellini, and
bring the soup back to a boil, stirring so tortellini will not stick to the
bottom. Continue boiling for 5 to 8 minutes until the soup is thick and
the tortellini are cooked. Remove and discard the bay leaves. Serve with
grated cheese at the table.

27
Egg Soup
Stracciatella

A classic peasant dish, this is egg-drop soup, Sicilian-style.
Stracciata means "shredded" and refers to the potatoes,
which are grated, as well as the eggs, which when scrambled
and poached seem shredded. Grate potatoes on the large
holes of a grater. The quantities of ingredients given in the
recipe below will make a main course for four. This soup is
deceptive: plain yet filling; really a winter food, but
appealing in the summer. You may want to try it as an
appetizer or for lunch. As a first course for four persons, use
exactly half the amounts listed below.

Serves 4

¼ teaspoon crushed red pepper flakes, or to taste

2 tablespoons (30 mL) olive oil

1 pound (454 g) potatoes, peeled and grated or sliced
   very fine

6 cups (1.4 L) Vegetable Broth (page 26)

Salt to taste

4 eggs, beaten

¼ cup (5 g) loosely packed finely chopped Italian parsley

Grated Parmesan for the table

In a heavy soup pot, heat the crushed red pepper in the olive oil over
medium heat. Add the potatoes and sauté briefly for a minute or two.
Add the broth and salt, and bring to a boil. Cover, lower heat, and cook
until potatoes are very soft, about 10 minutes.

Stir in the beaten eggs and the parsley and continue stirring for a minute or two until the eggs are thoroughly cooked. Serve hot with grated
cheese.

III
Pasta

Pasta is in many ways the "meat" of Italian cooking, in that meals often revolve around it. Sicilians generally use hard, egg-free macaroni that keeps its character in boiling water. Too often fresh pasta is soft and sometimes it is not very fresh. I recommend using good quality imported pasta.

It is very important to cook pasta correctly. Cooking times on packages are often unreliable. Place 1 pound of pasta in 6 quarts of rapidly boiling salted water. Test it periodically for doneness and drain it when it is still a bit undercooked and slightly wiry in the center. It continues cooking on its way to the table. If the recipe directions call for the pasta to be tossed with the sauce on a warm stove, you can drain it when it is slightly underdone, allowing the pasta to finish cooking by soaking up the juices in the sauce.

Always save some of the water that the pasta was cooked in. If the pasta is *too* underdone, you can always add the water a table-spoon or two at a time as you toss and stir the pasta with the sauce, as you would in making risotto—carefully controlling the cooking process in the final moments.

I am in the habit of rinsing all utensils and bowls used in making the sauce in the water that the pasta is to be cooked in, and adding to it a scrap or two of the vegetables or seasonings used in the sauce. For example, I rinse the pesto from the blade and bowl of the food processor with the pasta water; or, if I am making sauce with fresh rosemary and I have an extra sprig, I use it to perfume the water, discarding it after the pasta drains. This practice gives flavor to the pasta as it cooks, seasoning it subtly with the sauce before they actually join.

Instructions in the following recipes are for 1 pound (454 g) of pasta. This will serve 4 people as a main course.

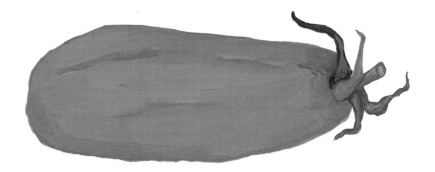

28
Linguine in Basic Tomato Sauce
Linguine con Salsa di Pomodoro

Use fresh ripe tomatoes when available. Skin them by placing them in boiling water for 20 seconds (see page 13). If you use canned tomatoes, use imported whole Italian plum tomatoes. Drain them well both before and after chopping. For extra flavor, instead of discarding the tomato juice, add it to the pasta water. If you like a thicker sauce add a small can (or part thereof) of tomato paste as the sauce cooks.

Serves 4: makes about 4 cups (946 mL) of sauce

Basic Tomato Sauce
2 cloves garlic, minced or crushed
¼ teaspoon crushed red pepper flakes, or to taste
¼ cup (59 mL) olive oil
3 to 4 pounds (1.4 to 1.8 kg) fresh tomatoes or 2 35-ounce
    (992 g) cans imported Italian plum tomatoes, chopped
2 tablespoons finely chopped Italian parsley
15 whole large basil leaves (or 1 teaspoon dried basil)
½ teaspoon dried oregano
Tomato paste (optional)
1 pound (454 g) linguine
Salt
Grated Parmesan for the table

Heat the garlic and pepper in the olive oil over high heat. When the oil begins to sizzle, add the tomatoes and stir. Add the parsley, basil, and oregano. Lower heat and cover, and simmer for 15 to 30 minutes.

Cook the pasta in salted water until it is al dente. Drain, return to the pot, and toss with 1 cup (237 mL) of the sauce. Spoon remaining sauce over the top of each portion and serve with grated cheese on the table.

29
Fusilli with Basil-Tomato Pesto
Fusilli con Pesto al Basilico e Pomodoro

Pesto means "ground." It is a sauce whose ingredients are crushed together. Traditionally, a mortar and pestle were used, but nowadays food processors and blenders make pesto preparation easy.

Besides adding an interesting twist to this popular sauce, the tomato enables you to use less oil. For traditional basil pesto, omit the tomato and add more olive oil to make the mixture blend together smoothly. One "bunch" of basil can vary considerably from another: you should have at least 2 cups (43 g) loosely packed. The more basil you use the richer the sauce, so since basil does not keep very well it makes sense to use any extra in your bunch, increasing the amounts of the other ingredients accordingly. The recipe below makes about enough to dress 1 pound (454 g) of pasta. Pesto sauce freezes well.

Serves 4

1 bunch basil leaves, washed well
½ pound (227 g) peeled tomatoes (see page 13)
¼ cup (5 g) Italian parsley
2 tablespoons (12 g) pine nuts
1 clove garlic
2 tablespoons (11 g) grated Parmesan, plus additional for the table
¼ teaspoon crushed red pepper flakes
3 tablespoons (44 mL) olive oil
1 pound (454 g) fusilli
Salt

Place all the ingredients, except for the fusilli and the grated cheese for the table, in a blender or food processor. Blend until the ingredients are smooth. If the mixture seems too thick, add more olive oil or chopped tomato. Transfer pesto to a bowl and keep in a warm place until ready to use. Cook fusilli in salted water until al dente. Gently toss with the sauce and serve with the extra cheese.

30
Farfalle with Sundried Tomato and Olive Pesto
Farfalle con Pesto al Pomodoro Secchi e Olivi

This pesto has a very strong flavor. It can be spread on bread, or used as a dressing for raw or cooked vegetables, but it is best on a short pasta such as *farfalle* or bow ties. The hotter the better, so add more crushed red pepper than ¼ teaspoon if you can take it.

Serves 4

8 sundried tomatoes packed in oil
8 salt-cured black olives, pitted
1 plum tomato, peeled (see page 13)
1 tablespoon (11 g) grated Parmesan, plus additional for the table
1 teaspoon dried rosemary, or 2 teaspoons fresh
8 basil leaves
2 sprigs Italian parsley
1 clove garlic
¼ teaspoon crushed red pepper flakes, or to taste
¼ cup (59 ml) olive oil
1 pound (454 g) *farfalle*
Salt

Place all ingredients in a blender or food processor and blend until smooth. If the consistency is too dry or thick, add more oil. Cook the *farfalle* in salted water until al dente. Toss with the sauce. Serve with grated Parmesan at the table.

31
Shells with Parsley Pesto
Conchiglie con Pesto Prezzemolo

This is Sicilian health food: reminiscent of tabouli salad, this pesto is as mild (yet zesty) as the preceding one is strong. It couldn't be easier to make, but you *must* use fresh green Italian parsley. This sauce is also very good as a dressing for raw or cooked vegetables.

Serves 4

2 cups (85 g) packed Italian parsley leaves
2 cloves garlic
¼ cup (59 mL) lemon juice
¼ cup (59 mL) olive oil
2 tablespoons chopped almonds
10 leaves fresh mint
Salt to taste
¼ teaspoon crushed red pepper flakes
1 pound (454 g) *conchiglie*
Grated Parmesan, pecorino, or locatalli cheese for the table
  (optional)

Place parsley, garlic, lemon juice, olive oil, almonds, mint leaves, salt, and crushed red pepper in a blender or food processor and process until smooth. Cook pasta in salted water until al dente. Drain, return to the pot, and toss with the pesto on the warm range. Serve with or without grated cheese.

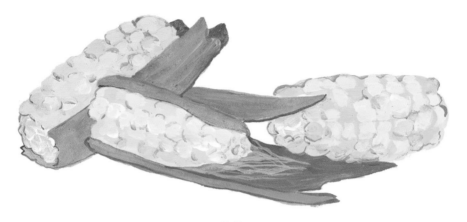

32
Orecchiette with Corn
Orecchiette al Adrano

Adrano is a town in the agricultural area near Mount Etna.
There, I sampled several pasta dishes which included fresh
corn off the cob. Fresh corn is somewhat unusual for Sicily
but as it is so common in America I put together what I
thought were the best elements of these recipes and came up
with this perfect light starter or side dish to be eaten in
August and September, when the corn is ripe and farm fresh.
With the addition of saffron the pasta becomes corn-yellow.
The shape of *orecchiette* catches the corn kernels, making this
a visually striking dish as well as a punning one—corn
coming off one ear and into another. If you cannot find
orecchiette try small shells or *cavatelli. Cavatelli* are short,
indented pasta, like shells except the dough is made with
fresh eggs and ricotta cheese as well as semolina flour.
Usually frozen, they are available in Italian groceries and
some supermarkets.

Serves 6 to 8 as an appetizer or side dish; 4 as a main dish

4 ears corn
Salt
2 tablespoons pine nuts
1 pound (454 g) *orecchiette*
½ gram saffron powder
¼ teaspoon crushed red pepper flakes
¼ cup (59 mL) olive oil
¼ cup (43 g) grated pecorino
¼ cup (57 g) roasted chopped red bell pepper (capsicum)
    (see page 25), about ¼ of a medium pepper

Shuck the corn, removing all the husks and silk. Break each cob in half. Bring 6 quarts (1.4 L) of salted water to a boil in a large pot and put in the corn. Remove from heat and let sit for a minute or two. Remove the ears from the pot and set them in a colander to drain and cool. Save the cooking water to cook the pasta. While corn is cooling, roast the pine nuts in a heavy pan over high heat, shaking and stirring them with a wooden spoon until they are toasted golden. Set aside.

Using a sharp knife, strip the kernels off the corncobs into a bowl and set aside. Bring the reserved pasta water back to a boil and add the *orecchiette*. Dissolve the saffron in ¼ cup (59 mL) of water from the pasta pot.

Meanwhile, in a separate pot, heat the crushed red pepper in the olive oil. When the oil is hot but not smoking, add the corn kernels, roasted bell pepper, and pine nuts. Stir over medium heat for 30 seconds.

When *orecchiette* is al dente, drain it, reserving some of the pasta water. Put the orecchiette in the pot with the corn. Add the dissolved saffron in its water and toss. Add the cheese a little at a time, mixing well, and adding a tablespoon or two of the reserved pasta water, if necessary, to make the mixing smoother. Serve immediately.

33
Quick Baked Vegetable Lasagna
Lasagna Pronto

If pasta is the meat of Italian cooking, lasagna is the sirloin—
a dish you eat with a knife and fork. You cannot say that
about many foods of grain origin. Because it uses uncooked
dried noodles, the following recipe is quick and easy, and
there is very little cleanup. The lasagna cooks in the oven by
absorbing the juices from the tomato sauce. You need a 10 by
12-inch (25 by 30 cm) heat-resistant glass or cast-iron baking
dish, or its equivalent, with a cover or with aluminum foil to
cover.

Serves 6

1 pound (454 g) ricotta

12 ounces (340 g) mozzarella, grated

½ cup (85 g) grated Parmesan, locatelli, or pecorino cheese

4 cups (946 mL) Basic Tomato Sauce (page 13)

1 pound (454 g) uncooked lasagna noodles

**2 cups (347 g) sliced and prepared vegetables (see below;
optional)**

Oregano

1 tablespoon (15 mL) olive oil (optional)

Preheat the oven to 350°F (180°C/gas 4).

Mix the ricotta with two thirds of the mozzarella and half of the Parmesan.

Oil the bottom and sides of the baking dish. Layer ingredients as follows: one fourth of the sauce, one third of the noodles (about 8), half of the cheese mixture, and half of the vegetables. Repeat for one more layer. Then, for the third and final layer, top with one fourth of the sauce, the final third of the noodles, then the final fourth of the sauce. Sprinkle the remaining mozzarella, Parmesan, and oregano to taste over all, and drizzle the oil over if you like a crusty top. Bake covered for 40 minutes, or until almost cooked through. Remove the cover and bake for an additional 15 minutes. Remove from oven and let stand 15 minutes before serving.

If you use vegetables, you can choose either a single one or a combination. Here are some suggestions: uncooked mushrooms, cut in thin slices; uncooked zucchini (courgettes), cut in thin slices; roasted red bell peppers (capsicums), sliced (see page 25); eggplant (aubergines), salted, drained, dusted with flour, and fried in olive oil; greens sautéed in olive oil until soft (see page 21); broccoli and/or cauliflower, parboiled and thinly sliced.

34

Baked Lasagna Noodles with Broccoli and Three Cheeses
Pasta al' Malfatti

Here, the lasagna is mixed together with the sauce and baked without regard to the symmetry or architecture of the dish. *Malfatti* means "badly made," and refers to the fact that the wide pasta is broken into odd shapes and baked with random layering.

Serves 4

1 head broccoli
Salt
3 cloves garlic, crushed or minced
¼ teaspoon crushed red pepper flakes, or to taste
¼ cup (59 mL) olive oil
1 pound (454 g) tomatoes, peeled and chopped (see page 13)
1 pound (454 g) uncooked lasagna noodles
2 ounces (57 g) goat cheese, crumbled
2 ounces (57 g) mozzarella, grated
½ cup (85 g) grated Parmesan, locatelli, or pecorino cheese

Remove the leaves and hard stem from the broccoli. Place the whole broccoli in a large pot with plenty of salted water to cover. Cook over high heat. When water comes to a boil, remove the broccoli. Save the water to cook the lasagna. Cut the broccoli into 1-inch (2.5 cm) or smaller florets.

In a large saucepan, heat the garlic and crushed red pepper in the olive oil over high heat. When the garlic begins to brown, add the broccoli and tomatoes. Stir briefly, then lower heat and simmer for 5 to 10 minutes or until broccoli is tender.

Preheat the oven to 400°F (200°C/gas 6).

Break lasagna noodles in half: the more noodles you break at a time, the more fragmenting you will get. Place broken noodles in boiling water and cook until al dente; some sticking together is inevitable and welcome. Drain noodles and mix them with the tomato and broccoli mixture. Place in a baking dish. Mix the cheeses together and sprinkle over the top. Bake in the oven for 10 minutes, or until the cheese melts and the edges of the noodles begin to turn brown. Serve immediately.

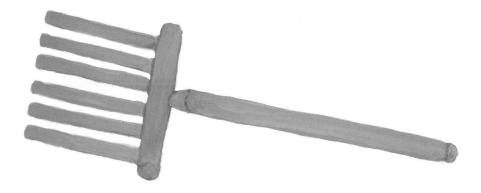

35
Linguine with Fennel
Pasta con Finocchi e Crostini

In this recipe you use the leafy green fennel tops as well as the bulb, so choose whole fennel. Make croutons by toasting two or three slices of your favorite Italian bread and cutting it into small squares.

Serves 4

1 bulb fennel, washed
1 clove garlic, pressed or finely minced
6 tablespoons (89 mL) olive oil
2 tablespoons (30 mL) white wine
½ cup (14 g) croutons
1 pound (454 g) linguine
Salt
2 tablespoons finely chopped Italian parsley
Ricotta salata for the table

Trim the base and hard stems from the fennel. Save about ¼ cup of the leaves, chop them finely, and set them aside. Cut the bulb horizontally into thin rounds, then dice. In a large heavy pot, heat the garlic in 5 tablespoons (74 mL) of olive oil. Add the sliced fennel bulb (not the leaves). Sauté about 2 minutes, until the fennel is coated with oil and begins to soften. Add the wine, lower the heat, cover, and simmer until the fennel is soft, about 5 minutes.

Meanwhile, sauté the croutons in the remaining olive oil, stirring to ensure they brown evenly. Place the linguine in boiling salted water. When it is al dente, drain it and place it in the pot with the fennel. Toss lightly. Add the croutons, parsley, and fennel tops. Mix thoroughly, warming through but not cooking the greens. Serve with grated *ricotta salata*.

36
Tortellini with Leeks, Fennel, and Cauliflower
Tortellini con Porri, Finocchio, e Cavolfiore

This is a medley of sweet vegetables. Save some fennel
leaves, chopped small, for the garnish.

Serves 4

1 small head cauliflower, enough to yield 2 cups (347 g)
  cooked florets
4 leeks
1 bulb fennel
6 tablespoons (89 mL) olive oil
¼ teaspoon crushed red pepper flakes, or to taste
1 tablespoon (15 mL) freshly squeezed lemon juice
2 pounds (907 g) cheese tortellini
Salt
Grated Parmesan for the table

Wash the cauliflower and place it whole in a large pot. Fill with water, cover, bring to a boil, and cook for 7 minutes or until head is soft but not falling apart. Remove cauliflower from the pot. Save the water for the tortellini. Cut into 1-inch (2.5 cm) florets.

Trim the leeks' bottoms and tops. Discard the top layer, and the next if it is fibrous. Leeks get sandy, so wash them well. Slice them in half lengthwise and rinse between the layers. Dry, and cut into 1-inch (2.5 cm) pieces.

Remove the bottom and the top from the fennel bulb. Discard the hard outer layer. Slice the bulb horizontally in ½-inch (1 cm) slices, then chop the slices into 1-inch (2.5 cm) pieces. Save the leafy green fennel tops for garnish.

Heat the oil and crushed red pepper in a heavy pot over medium high heat. Add the leeks and sauté until transparent, about 2 minutes. Add the fennel and sauté until transparent. Add the cauliflower and quickly stir-fry for about another 2 minutes. Add ¼ cup (59 mL) of the reserved cauliflower cooking water, lower heat, and cover. Simmer slowly for about 5 minutes. Stir in the lemon juice and keep warm while you cook the pasta.

Lightly salt the remaining cauliflower cooking water and bring it to a boil and place tortellini in it. Salt to taste. When they rise to the top, test one to make sure it's done. Drain, and gently toss the tortellini with the vegetables. Garnish with the reserved fennel leaves and serve with grated Parmesan.

37
Penne with White Beans and Mushrooms
Penne con Fagioli e Funghi

This recipe can be made meatier by using dried porcini mushrooms (ceps) instead of fresh portabellos. Start with 1½ ounces (21 g) of dried porcinis and soak them for ½ hour with the peeled and chopped tomato in 2 tablespoons (30 mL) of red wine. If you are using dried porcinis, you may need to simmer this sauce a little longer to cook the mushrooms. You can use either dry or canned cannellini beans; if you are using dried beans, soak overnight and boil for 1 hour.

Serves 4

1 red bell pepper (capsicum)
1 pound (454 g) portabello mushrooms
1 large clove garlic, pressed or minced
¼ teaspoon crushed red pepper flakes, or to taste
6 tablespoons (89 mL) olive oil
½ cup (149 g) peeled and chopped tomato (see page 13)
2 cups (340 g) cooked cannellini beans, or one 19-ounce (538 g) can, drained
¼ cup (5 g) loosely packed chopped Italian parsley
1 pound (454 g) penne
10 fresh basil leaves, chopped
Grated Parmesan, locatelli, or pecorino cheese for the table

Roast the pepper as on page 25, skin, cut into long strips and set aside. Cut off mushroom stems and slice caps into 1 by 2-inch (2.5 by 5 cm) strips. Heat the garlic and the crushed red pepper in the olive oil over medium heat. Add the mushroom slices and sauté for a minute or two until they start to soften. Add the peppers, tomato, and beans, lower heat, and simmer for 5 minutes. Keep warm while you cook the pasta.

In boiling, lightly salted water, cook penne until al dente. Drain and mix with the beans and mushrooms. Add the basil and parsley and gently stir on a warm stove until all liquid is absorbed. Serve with grated cheese.

38
Spaghetti with Peas
Pasta e Piselli

For this quickly made sauce, fresh peas are best—if they are really fresh. The sugar in peas starts turning to starch and the skins start getting tough as soon as the peas are taken from the vine. If it is not springtime and you are not on a farm or near one, use fancy grade frozen baby peas.

Serves 4

¼ teaspoon crushed red pepper flakes, or to taste

⅓ cup (78 mL) olive oil

3 shallots, chopped very fine

3 plum tomatoes, peeled and chopped (see page 13)

2 cups (369 g) baby peas (thawed if frozen)

1 red bell pepper (capsicum) roasted (see page 25), diced small

3 sundried tomatoes packed in oil, chopped small

¼ teaspoon nutmeg

1 pound (454 g) spaghetti

Salt to taste

Grated Parmesan, locatelli, or pecorino cheese for the table

Heat the crushed red pepper in the olive oil over medium-high heat. Add the shallots and sauté until they are soft, about 4 to 5 minutes, stirring so they will not burn. Add the plum tomatoes and stir for 1 minute. Add the peas, roasted pepper, sundried tomatoes, and nutmeg. Gently stir again over medium heat for a minute or so until peas are mixed in and warmed through.

Boil pasta in salted water until al dente. Drain well, return to the pot, and gently toss with the sauce over low heat until all liquids are absorbed into the pasta. Serve hot with plenty of grated cheese.

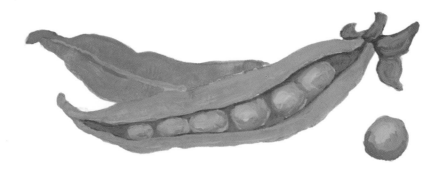

39
Fettucine with Arugula and Goat Cheese
Fettucini con Rughetta e Formaggio Caprino

Southern Italians rarely eat heavy cream with their pasta,
Sicilians never, although they do on occasion melt goat
cheese or fresh ricotta for a slightly creamy pasta dish. This
satisfying dish couldn't be simpler. Try a ripe goat cheese
such as *bûcheron*.

Serves 4

¼ teaspoon crushed red pepper flakes, or to taste

¼ cup (59 mL) olive oil

2 large bunches arugula (rocket), coarse stems removed,
washed, dried, and chopped small

1 pound (454 g) fettucine

Salt

4 ounces (113 g) goat cheese

Grated Parmesan, pecorino, or locatelli cheese for the table
(optional)

Heat the crushed red pepper in the olive oil over high heat. When it
is sizzling hot add the arugula, stirring until it is reduced and soft, about
1 minute.

Boil the fettucine in salted water until al dente. Save a little pasta water
in a cup. Drain, return the pasta to the pot, and toss in the arugula. Over
low heat, add the goat cheese and mix thoroughly, adding the reserved
pasta water a tablespoon or two at a time as needed to make the mixing
easier if it seems too stiff. Serve hot—with or without grated cheese,
according to taste.

40
Farfalle with Rosemary and Saffron
Farfalle con Rosamarino e Zafferano

This dish's yellow bowties are dramatic and different. It's an
elegant pasta that is perhaps more suited as a starter or side
dish because of its subtlety and simplicity. Fresh rosemary is
a must. Steamed chopped asparagus spears or sautéed sliced
artichokes can be added if you want a more substantial dish.

Serves 6 to 8

¼ cup (14 g) very finely chopped fresh rosemary leaves
¼ cup (59 mL) olive oil
¼ cup (59 mL) dry white wine
1 pound (454 g) *farfalle*
Salt
¼ gram saffron powder

Heat the rosemary in the olive oil gently over low heat for a few minutes, until the oil is infused with the rosemary's aromatic perfume. Add
the wine, cover, and cook slowly for 10 minutes.

Set the *farfalle* to boil in salted water. When it is half-cooked, scoop
out ¼ cup (59 mL) of the pasta water and dissolve the saffron in it. Continue cooking the pasta until it is al dente. Drain, return to the pot,
and toss with the sauce on a warm stove. Add the saffron water and mix
thoroughly. Serve hot.

41
Penne in Hot Pink Sauce
Penne all'Inferno

A sweet and hot Sicilian version of the Florentine specialty
penne with vodka sauce. Amaro is a Sicilian liqueur, like
Fernet-Branca but not so bitter. It is the ideal Sicilian dessert
liqueur, and worth looking for. Most large liquor stores carry
it. If you cannot find amaro, substitute Grand Marnier. Use
more crushed red pepper if you can take it.

Serves 4

1 28-ounce (227 g) can of Italian plum tomatoes packed
    with basil (see page 13)

½ teaspoon crushed red pepper flakes, or to taste

2 cloves garlic, pressed or minced

¼ cup (59 mL) olive oil

1 pound (454 g) penne

Salt

2 tablespoons (30 mL) amaro liqueur or Grand Marnier

½ cup (113 g) ricotta

¼ cup (5 g) loosely packed finely chopped Italian parsley
    leaves

Drain the tomatoes. Chop them and drain them again (tomato juice
can be put in the pasta water). Heat the crushed red pepper and garlic
in the olive oil in a large heavy pot over high heat. When the garlic is
sizzling and brown, but before it burns, add the tomatoes. Stir, reduce
heat, cover, and cook for about 10 minutes, or until tomatoes begin to
liquefy.

Cook the penne in salted water, with reserved tomato juice added,
until al dente. Drain and return to the pot. Over low heat, mix the pasta
with the tomato sauce. Add the liqueur, the ricotta, and the parsley, and
toss. Let sit over low heat for a few minutes, stirring occasionally, until
all liquid is absorbed into the pasta before serving.

42

Spaghetti with Broccoli Pesto
Pasta con Pesto al Broccoli

This simple but flavorful dish becomes dramatic with the addition of extra crushed red pepper or more garlic.

Serves 4

1 head broccoli, cut or broken into stems
Salt
2 cloves garlic, or to taste, pressed or minced
½ teaspoon crushed red pepper flakes, or to taste
6 tablespoons (89 mL) olive oil
1 pound (454 g) spaghetti
Grated Parmesan, locatelli, or pecorino cheese for the table

Cut bottoms from the broccoli stems. Place broccoli tops in cold water in a large pot, add salt, cover, and bring to a boil. Lower heat and simmer for 3 or 4 minutes. Remove broccoli from the pot and drain, saving the water to boil the pasta.

Cut the cooked broccoli tops into small florets. Skin what remains of the stems and chop small.

Heat the garlic and crushed red pepper in the oil over high heat. When the garlic browns and the pepper sizzles, add the chopped broccoli. Stir to coat garlic, pepper, and broccoli with oil. Add ¼ cup (59 mL) of water from the pasta pot. Lower the heat to medium, cover, and cook for 15 to 20 minutes, or until the broccoli is very soft, adding a tablespoon or two of the reserved broccoli cooking water if it becomes too dry.

Bring the broccoli cooking water to a boil and cook the spaghetti until it is just short of al dente. Drain, reserving some water in a cup, and return the spaghetti to the pot. Over low heat, mix the underdone spaghetti with the broccoli sauce, adding a tablespoon or two of the reserved water if necessary. Continue to stir for about 2 minutes, until all liquid is absorbed and the pasta is cooked. Serve with grated cheese if desired.

43

Cheese Ravioli with Olives, Tomatoes, Potatoes, and Almonds
Ravioli alla Ghiota

The fantasy: homemade ravioli. The reality: unless you have the right touch, homemade ravioli, if they fall apart in the boiling water, can be disastrous. Many store-bought ravioli, even the expensive kind sold in luxury food stores, do the same, no matter how briefly or gently you cook them. If you are lucky enough to live near an Italian store that specializes in ravioli, you will undoubtedly find a high quality product. Otherwise, the frozen brands that have been on the market for decades are the most reliable. Keep them frozen until ready to boil.

If you use frozen ravioli, small ravioli (fifty per pound) are recommended for the following recipe. Pasta in a potato sauce is called *alla ghiota*, "glutton's style." In fact, though it seems unusual, this tasty peasant sauce is an economical energy food. Use a blender or food processor to grind the almonds.

Serves 4 heavy eaters

Fresh Ravioli

2 cups (370 g) semolina flour

1 egg, beaten

½ cup (118 mL) warm water

Ricotta cheese and/or cooked vegetables for filling

Cornmeal for dusting

2 cloves garlic, crushed or minced

¼ teaspoon crushed red pepper flakes, or to taste

¼ cup (59 mL) olive oil

2 pounds (907 g) tomatoes, peeled and chopped (see page 13)

10 black olives packed in oil, pitted and minced

1 pound (454 g) potatoes, peeled and sliced in thin circles or semi-circles (imitate the shape of your ravioli)

¼ cup (57 g) finely ground almonds

½ cup (118 mL) dry white wine

¼ cup (5 g) chopped loosely packed Italian parsley leaves

¼ teaspoon nutmeg

2 pounds (907 g) cheese ravioli, fresh or frozen

Grated Parmesan, pecorino, or locatelli cheese for the table

To make the ravioli, combine the semolina flour, egg, and water and mix until you have a smooth dough. Knead until it is elastic. If it is too dry, add more water; if too wet, add more flour. Divide and roll into sheets ⅛ inch (.3 cm) thick. Cut them into 2-inch (5 cm) squares. Put a heaping teaspoon of filling (ricotta only, or any cooked vegetable and cheese) on half of the squares. Place the remaining squares over the filling and seal all edges well with a fork. Set on a plate or board dusted with cornmeal. Cook gently for a minute or so in a large pot of boiling water.

To make the sauce, heat the garlic, crushed red pepper, and olive oil in a saucepot over high heat until they sizzle. Add the tomatoes and olives and sauté a minute over high heat. Add the potatoes and sauté another minute. Add the almonds, wine, parsley, and nutmeg. Lower heat and simmer for ½ hour to 40 minutes, until the potatoes are quite soft.

Place the ravioli in a large pot of gently boiling water. Stir occasionally to keep the ravioli from sticking together or to the bottom. After all the ravioli rise to the surface, continue to cool for a minute or two. The only way to tell if they are done is to taste one. Drain and serve with grated cheese.

44

Penne with Tomato, Basil, Fried Eggplant, and Ricotta Salata
Penne alla Norma

Pasta with eggplant (aubergine) is often called "alla Norma." Some say that the name is derived from Bellini's opera, *Norma*, and that it reflects the composer's love of eggplant. It is more likely to mean "normal" or "the usual," as pasta with eggplant is a Sicilian staple.

Serves 4

1 large eggplant (aubergine), about 1 pound (454 g)
Salt
1 pound (454 g) tomatoes, peeled and chopped (see page 13)
20 fresh basil leaves
¼ cup (5 g) loosley packed chopped Italian parsley
¼ teaspoon crushed red pepper flakes, or to taste
½ cup (118 mL) olive oil
1 pound (454 g) penne
4 ounces (113 g) *ricotta salata* (see page 42), grated or crumbled, for garnish

Peel the eggplant, cut into ½-inch (1 cm) cubes, salt generously, and let sit in a colander for an hour.

Mix the tomatoes in a bowl with the basil leaves, parsley, salt to taste, and crushed red pepper. Set aside. Heat the olive oil in a medium skillet on high heat. Gently squeeze the excess moisture out of the eggplant cubes and fry them in the oil, browning on all sides. Set aside.

In boiling, salted water, cook the penne until it is just short of al dente. Drain and return to the pot. Add the tomato-basil mixture and the fried eggplant with a tablespoon or two of the olive oil. Stir over low heat a minute or so until all the ingredients are warmed and the pasta, absorbing the tomato's juices, is cooked.

Garnish each portion with cheese; have extra cheese on the table.

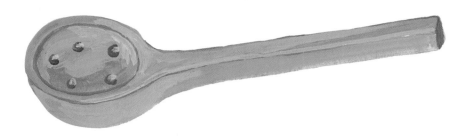

45

Gnocchi
Gnocchi di Patati

Gnocchi are wheat and potato pasta dumplings. They are not
native to Sicily, but are a Roman specialty that has found its
way south. A welcome change from all-semolina pasta,
gnocchi are interesting in themselves, and best served with
simple sauces such as Basil Pesto (page 49), Basic Tomato
Sauce (page 48), or tossed with garlic and Sautéed Spinach
(page 21). Gnocchi are available frozen or refrigerated in
most Italian stores and some supermarkets. Although I
recommend that you buy packaged ravioli, gnocchi are never
as good as when you make them yourself—and they are
virtually foolproof. Perhaps because each little dumpling is
slightly different in size and shape, they give the meal a
rustic elegance.

Serves 4

1 pound (454 g) potatoes
1 egg, beaten
¼ cup (43 g) grated Parmesan, plus additional for the table
Pinch of salt
¼ teaspoon nutmeg
1 cup (184 g) semolina flour or unbleached white flour

Peel the potatoes, cut them in quarters, and boil them in water to cover
for 15 minutes or until they are cooked. Drain and let them cool, then
mash them with a potato masher or a fork. Small lumps don't matter.
Add the egg, cheese, salt, and nutmeg and mix thoroughly. Add the flour
a little at a time until you have a stiff dough. If it is too dry, add more
water; if too wet, add more flour. Pull off a piece that will fit in the palm
of your hand and roll it out between your palms until it is a long cylinder
about ¾ inch (2 cm) thick, like a long bread stick. Cut it into ½-inch
(4 cm) lengths, smoothing the ends with floured hands. With your little
finger, press the center of each gnocchi, making a slight dent. This will
help them catch the sauce.

Place gnocchi on a floured board, plate, or waxed paper (greaseproof).

When all the gnocchi are formed, bring water to a boil in a large pot
and place them in it. Stir gently to keep gnocchi from sticking to the
bottom. When they rise to the surface and the water is again at a rapid
boil, they are done. Serve with sauce and cheese.

IV
Rice
Riso

As Milan has exported its style worldwide, many of its culinary specialties have become very chic, arriving in America along with expensive shoes and knits. In recent years, risotto has been appearing on Sicilian menus, along with traditional favorites such as Rice Pie (page 80), *Arancini* (page 78), and the rice pilafs left behind from Turkish invasions (see pages 75 and 76). Like polenta and other northern Italian dishes, risotto or *risuttu* as it is called in Sicily, though still viewed suspiciously, is slowly gaining acceptance. For all its well-heeled mystique, risotto can be a simply delicious dish of rice and vegetables prepared in the elegant and rustic Sicilian manner.

To prepare risotto properly, you must start with the short-grain, high-gluten rice called Arborio, grown in the Po Valley in northern Italy. You can find it in Italian stores, specialty shops, and large supermarkets. This high-starch grain is both firm and creamy when it is cooked. If you wash the rice before using it, your rice will not be as creamy. Arborio rice is recommended, for its taste and texture, in all the recipes in this book.

To start, three risotto recipes are offered. Let them serve as guides to your imagination for all the different risottos you can make by using various vegetables, herbs, and other ingredients. Try risotto with dried porcini mushrooms or fresh mushrooms, green beans, peas, broccoli, cauliflower, spinach, radicchio, sun-dried tomatoes, any cheese, pine nuts, currants, olives, almonds, artichokes, arugula (rocket), leeks, zucchini (courgettes), saffron, basil, garlic, rosemary, oregano, tomatoes, bell peppers (capsicums), onions, eggplant (aubergines), carrots, beets (a fun color), pumpkin, Savoy cabbage, fava beans, you name it. Generally it is better for the vegetables and the rice to be cooked together so the flavors can mix. However, as in the case of greens, which cook quickly, some ingredients should be prepared separately and added to the rice at the end of cooking, so they will not be over-done. Let your common sense dictate.

Risotto is quick to make but you must pay careful attention to it, especially the first few times. Be organized! Use a heavy 4- or 5-quart (about 4 or 5 L) pot for the rice. Have the broth at a low boil in another pot, the measuring cup handy, and an easy-to-read clock within range. The perfect risotto is done in 18 minutes, but there are many factors. If the heat under the rice is the right degree of "medium" it should take about 2 minutes before you are ready to add the next ½ cup (118 mL) of broth to the rice. You do not want to cool the rice too much when you add liquid, so if your time varies, adjust the amount of broth you are adding or the heat on your stove.

Generally, for cooking rice, the ratio of liquid to rice is 2 to 1. However, with risotto, since there is evaporation, and the finished product is meant to be velvety and a bit liquid, that ratio is more like 3 to 1. The quality of different brands of rice varies. Some absorb a little more and some a little less broth. Obviously, if 16 minutes have passed and the rice is done, even if you have not used all the broth or liquid, stop cooking. If, as is less likely, after 18 minutes you have used all the broth and there is a dry spot in the center of the risotto, add small quantities of boiling water and continue cooking until it is cooked through. Just remember, don't add more liquid until you see that what you have already added has been absorbed.

If all goes well the rice will be both tender and firm and creamy, with each grain separate and uniformly cooked. But all this is not as complicated as it sounds—just pay attention, and remember, you are only cooking rice.

46
Rice with Fennel and Parsley
Risotto con Finocchio e Prezzemolo

This risotto is light, sweet, and delicious.

Serves 4

4½ cups (1.1 L) Vegetable Broth (page 36)
2 tablespoons (28 g) unsalted butter
2 tablespoons (30 mL) olive oil
½ cup (78 g) finely minced onion
1 fresh fennel bulb, trimmed, cut into thin slices and diced into ½–inch (1 cm) pieces (about 1 cup)
1½ cups (340 g) Arborio rice
½ cup (118 mL) dry white wine
1 cup (21 g) loosely packed Italian parsley leaves
¼ cup (43 g) grated Parmesan, pecorino, or locatelli cheese
2 tablespoons finely minced fennel leaves

Bring the broth to a boil, lower the heat, and keep it simmering slowly on the stove.

In a heavy pot over medium heat, melt half of the butter in the olive oil. Add the onion and sauté until transparent and soft, about 5 minutes. Be careful not to brown or burn the onion.

Add the chopped fennel bulb and stir for 2 minutes. Add the rice. Using a wooden spoon, turn it gently in the pot for about a minute until all the grains are coated. Do not sear. Add the wine and stir until it is entirely absorbed.

Add ¾ cup of the parsley leaves, and ½ cup (118 mL) of the broth, stirring constantly to prevent sticking. When the broth is completely absorbed, repeat the process, adding broth by the ½ cup (118 mL) until the rice is cooked, about 18 minutes.

Add the other half of the butter. Stir in the grated cheese, fennel leaves, and the remaining parsley leaves. Serve immediately.

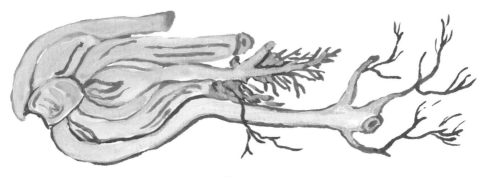

47

Rice with Tomatoes, Basil, and Mozzarella
Risotto alla Margarita

This is like pizza rice. The liquid in the tomatoes reduces
the amount of broth needed. The mozzarella does get
stringy; for a different texture and taste you may substitute
fontina, provolone, goat cheese, or extra grated Parmesan.

Serves 4

3⅓ cups (788 mL) Vegetable Broth (page 36)

2 tablespoons (28 g) unsalted butter

2 tablespoons (30 mL) olive oil

¼ teaspoon crushed red pepper flakes, or to taste

¼ cup (37 g) minced onion

1½ cups (340 g) Arborio rice

1 cup (237 mL) peeled and chopped tomatoes (see page 13)

⅓ cup (78 mL) dry red wine

1 teaspoon dried oregano

20 large basil leaves

¼ cup (43 g) grated Parmesan

4 ounces (113 g) mozzarella, cut into tiny cubes

Salt to taste

Bring the broth to a boil, lower the heat, and keep simmering slowly
on the stove.

In a heavy pot, melt half of the butter in the olive oil. Add the crushed
red pepper and the onion and sauté for a few minutes until the onion
softens and becomes transparent, about 5 minutes. Be careful not to
burn it.

Add the rice. Stir gently for a few moments, so that all the grains are
well coated with oil and butter. Add the tomatoes and wine and stir until
the liquid is absorbed. Add ⅓ cup (78 mL) of the broth, and stir until it
also is absorbed. Repeat the process, adding ⅓ cup of the broth every
couple of minutes until the rice is cooked, about 18 minutes.

Remove the risotto from the heat. Add the other half of the butter,
the oregano, and the basil leaves. Stir in the Parmesan, then stir in the
mozzarella a little at a time so it will not all stick together. Add salt to
taste and serve immediately.

48
Rice with Asparagus and Mushrooms
Risotto al Aspergi e Porcini

The "green" flavor of the asparagus contrasts with the earthiness of the mushrooms. The tips of the asparagus should be al dente, the stems well-cooked. If you have very young and tender asparagus, you may want to add the tips at the last minute.

Serves 4

½ ounce (14 g) dried porcini mushrooms (ceps)
1 cup (248 g) peeled and chopped tomatoes (see page 13)
3½ cups (828 mL) Vegetable Broth (page 36)
2 tablespoons (28 g) unsalted butter
2 tablespoons (30 mL) olive oil
1 onion, finely chopped
1 clove garlic, minced
1 pound (454 g) asparagus, trimmed, peeled, and cut into
    1-inch (2.5 cm) pieces, with tips kept separate
1½ cups (340 g) Arborio rice
½ cup (118 mL) dry white wine
2 tablespoons finely chopped Italian parsley
2 tablespoons (21 g) grated Parmesan

Cut the mushrooms into pieces, mix with the chopped tomatoes, and set aside. Bring the broth to a boil, lower the heat, and keep it simmering slowly on the stove.

In a heavy pot, melt half the butter in the olive oil over medium heat. Add the onion and garlic and sauté until the onion is transparent, about 5 minutes. Add the asparagus stems and sauté for 1 minute. Add the rice, stirring for about 1 minute to coat it well with oil and butter.

Add the tomato and mushroom mixture and stir for another minute, letting the rice absorb the tomato liquid. Add the wine and stir until it is also completely absorbed. Start adding the broth ½ cup (118 mL) at a time, stirring constantly and letting the rice absorb the liquid before adding more. After 14 minutes, add the asparagus tops. Continue adding the broth until the rice is cooked, about 18 minutes. Remove from the heat. Add the remaining butter, the parsley, and the Parmesan. Mix well and serve immediately.

49
Rice Pilaf with Mushrooms
Riso Pilau con Funghi

Pilaf was originally a Turkish dish and it is much more common in Sicily than risotto is. It is considerably easier and requires little—rather than constant—attention. Use Arborio rice for best results.

Serves 4

2½ cups (591 mL) Vegetable Broth (page 36)

1 tablespoon (14 g) butter

5 tablespoons (74 mL) olive oil

1 pound (454 g) portabello mushrooms, washed and dried, stems cut off, and cut into 1-inch (2.5 cm) pieces

¼ teaspoon crushed red pepper flakes, or to taste

4 shallots, minced

1½ cups (340 g) Arborio rice

¼ cup (46 g) pine nuts

1 tablespoon currants

½ teaspoon grated orange peel

⅓ gram saffron powder

½ cup (118 mL) white wine

Salt to taste

Bring the broth to a boil, lower the heat, and keep it simmering slowly on the stove.

In a heavy pot, melt the butter in 3 tablespoons (44 mL) of the olive oil over medium-high heat. Add the mushrooms and sauté about 3 minutes, until the mushrooms are soft but not underdone. Remove from pot and set aside. In the same pot, heat the crushed red pepper in the remaining 2 tablespoons (30 mL) of olive oil. Add the shallots and cook over medium heat about 2 minutes, until shallots are soft. Do not let them burn.

Add the rice, pine nuts, currants, and orange peel. Stir until all are thoroughly coated with the oil, about 1 minute. Dissolve the saffron in the wine. Add this to the pot along with the hot broth, and salt. Reduce heat to low, cover, and simmer for 10 minutes. Add the mushrooms, stir, and cover again. Cook an additional 5 minutes. Remove from heat and let sit covered 3 to 5 minutes before serving.

50
Rice Pilaf with Sundried Tomatoes and Roasted Peppers
Pilau al'Caltagirone

This is piquant rice dish. Some crushed red pepper guidelines: ¼ teaspoon is zestful, ½ teaspoon is getting fierce, ¾ teaspoon or more is for hardline hotheads. If hot chile peppers are available, substitute them for the dried pepper.

Serves 4

1½ cups (355 mL) tomato juice or Vegetable
  Broth (page 36)
Crushed red pepper flakes to taste
3 tablespoons (44 mL) olive oil
1 cup (156 g) minced onion
1½ cups (340 g) Arborio rice
¼ cup (46 g) pine nuts
½ cup (118 mL) dry white wine
Salt to taste
8 black olives packed in oil, pitted and chopped
½ pound (227 g) sundried tomatoes packed in oil, chopped in
  quarters
1 large red bell pepper (capsicum), roasted and cut in thin
  slices (see page 25)

Dilute the tomato juice with 1 cup (237 mL) of water and bring to a slow boil. In a heavy pot, heat crushed red pepper in the olive oil over medium-high heat. Add the onions and sauté 3 to 5 minutes or until they soften. Do not let them burn. Add the rice and the pine nuts, stirring constantly for a minute or two, so that each grain and nut is thoroughly coated with the oil. Add the wine, then the broth or water and tomato juice, and salt. Cover and cook 10 minutes over low heat.

Stir in the olives, sundried tomatoes, and red pepper slices. Cover and cook for an additional 5 minutes. Remove from heat and let sit covered another 3 to 5 minutes before serving.

51
Rice Balls
Arancini

Arancini means "little oranges"; perhaps this is due both to
these balls' size and to the saffron and tomato that makes
them orange inside.

Makes 8 balls: serves 8 as an appetizer or side dish, 4 as a
main course

1 ounce (28 g) dried porcini mushrooms, chopped
1 28-ounce (227 g) can crushed tomatoes
1 cup (237 mL) tomato juice
2 tablespoons (30 mL) olive oil
1½ cups (340 g) Arborio rice
1 tablespoon (14 g) butter
Salt to taste
¼ gram saffron powder
1 clove garlic, crushed or minced
¼ teaspoon crushed red pepper flakes, or to taste
1 cup (156 g) minced onion
1 cup (184 g) fresh or frozen baby peas (if frozen, thawed to
    room temperature)
3 eggs
½ cup (86 g) grated pecorino
½ cup (43 g) grated provolone
8 pine nuts (optional)
8 raisins (sultanas)
½ cup (118 mL) unbleached all-purpose (plain) flour
1 cup (128 g) unseasoned dried bread crumbs (see page 28)
Vegetable oil for frying (olive oil mixed half-and-half with
    soybean, corn, or safflower oil), enough to come to ½ inch
    (1 cm) deep in the drying pan

Combine the mushrooms and crushed tomatoes and set aside. Dilute the tomato juice with 2 cups (473 mL) of water and bring to a boil on the stove.

In a heavy pot with a lid, heat half the olive oil. Add the rice, stirring constantly to coat the grains with oil. Add the boiling water and tomato juice to the rice along with the butter, salt, and saffron. Cover, lower heat, and cook for 15 minutes. Remove from heat and let sit covered until the rice is cool enough to handle, about an hour.

Meanwhile, heat the remaining olive oil in a sauce pot. Add the garlic, crushed red pepper, and onion. Sauté until the onion is soft, about 5 minutes. Add the tomatoes and mushrooms. Bring to a boil, lower heat, cover, and simmer for 15 minutes. Add the peas and remove from the heat.

Beat one egg and add it to the rice, along with the pecorino and provolone. Form the rice into a symmetrical pie shape that will allow you to divide it into 8 even amounts.

Wet your hands with cold water, pick up one eighth of the rice and form into a ball. Press your index finger into the ball as far as it will go without coming out the other side. Fill the resulting hole with a few teaspoons of the "sauce" (use more peas and mushrooms than sauce). Reshape the ball, sealing the sauce, peas, and mushrooms inside. Place on a floured board, waxed paper (greaseproof), or a dish.

Repeat until you have rolled up all 8 balls. (For a sweet variation, add a pine nut and a raisin to each.) When you have formed all the balls, roll them in flour. Beat the remaining 2 eggs in a bowl and dip the rice balls in the eggs, then roll them in the bread crumbs.

In a heavy frying pan, heat the oil until it is quite hot but not burning. Put the rice balls in gently, rolling them until they are golden brown on all sides. Remove them with a metal slotted spoon or two forks and let them drain on paper towels or brown paper.

Reheat the remaining sauce. Serve the rice balls whole, with the sauce on the table, or cut the balls in half with a very sharp knife and serve with a few spoons of sauce on each.

52

Rice Pie
Riso al Forno

If you like, you can substitute a pound of sliced, sautéed mushrooms for the eggplant (aubergine). Use an 8 by 10-inch (20 by 25 cm) baking dish, a 10-inch (25 cm) round cast-iron skillet, or their equivalent.

Serves 4 as a main dish

1 cup (237 mL) tomato juice (if you use canned tomatoes, use the juice you drain)
¼ cup (59 mL) olive oil
1½ cups (340 g) Arborio rice
1 tablespoon (14 g) butter
Salt
1½ pounds (681 g) eggplant (aubergine)
1 onion, minced
1 clove garlic, pressed or minced
¼ teaspoon crushed red pepper flakes, or to taste
1 pound (454 g) fresh or canned tomatoes, peeled and chopped (see page 13)
2 tablespoons (32 g) tomato paste
½ cup (92 g) unbleached all-purpose (plain) flour
Vegetable oil for frying eggplant, enough to come to a generous ¼ inch (.6 cm) deep in the pan
2 eggs, beaten
½ cup (85 g) grated pecorino
½ cup (43 g) grated provolone
2 tablespoons (28 g) ground almonds
¼ cup (5 g) loosely packed chopped Italian parsley leaves
¾ cup (96 g) unseasoned dried bread crumbs (see page 13)

Dilute the tomato juice in 2 cups (473 mL) of water and bring to a slow boil.

In a separate pot with a heavy lid, heat 1 teaspoon (15 mL) of the olive oil. Add the rice and stir over medium heat for 1 minute, until rice grains are coated with oil. Pour in the boiling water and tomato juice. Add the butter and salt, lower heat, cover, and cook for 15 minutes. Remove pot from heat and let sit, covered, until rice reaches room temperature, about 1 hour.

Meanwhile, peel the eggplant and slice it into ½-inch (1 cm) rounds. Salt generously and let the slices sit in a colander to drain for about 30 minutes.

To make the sauce, sauté the onion, garlic, and crushed red pepper in the remaining olive oil until the onion is soft, about 5 minutes. Add the chopped tomatoes and tomato paste and bring to a boil. Lower heat, cover, and simmer for 15 minutes.

Squeeze the eggplant slices gently to remove excess moisture. Coat the slices in flour and fry them in vegetable oil, browning them on both sides. Remove from pan with a metal slotted spoon or two forks and let them drain on paper towels.

Preheat the oven to 375°F (190°C/gas 5).

Add the eggs, half of the pecorino, the provolone, ground almonds, and parsley to the rice and mix thoroughly. Oil the bottom of a baking dish or cast-iron skillet. Place half the rice on the bottom of the pan. Layer the eggplant slices over the rice, overlapping slices if necessary. Then cover with 1 cup (237 mL) of the sauce (use more if you like). Spoon the other half of the rice on top of the sauce. Mix the remaining pecorino with the bread crumbs and spread the mixture over the rice. Bake until the top is brown, about 30 minutes.

Serve with the remaining sauce on the table.

V
Polenta

Northern Italians call Sicilians *terroni:* earth people or peasants. Sicilians have been known to use stronger language to strike back. One of the milder epithets is *polentoni*, corn-mush people. The connotation is that northerners are mealy-mouthed and lack the guts and the gusto of people from the south. But there is no room in a united Italy for food chauvinism, and in fact, when prepared with *Sicilianismo*, cornmeal can be almost as satisfying as pasta.

Cornmeal is available in every supermarket. Most is degerminated and enriched, which means it has had vitamins and minerals taken out in the milling and replaced artificially. Nondegerminated polenta has a stronger flavor and is available in health food stores. It can be used instead of the refined meal if you prefer a more earthy dish. In Italian stores you will find a variety of finer and coarser grinds. Some cooks say that one should only use the finer grind when making polenta as a cereal; otherwise, use the coarse meal. However, in practice, there should be no hard and fast rule. Personally, I prefer combining fine and coarse degerminated and nondegerminated. As with many choices in the art of cooking, the mixture seems to give the best of both worlds.

As with rice and pasta, polenta goes with almost any food you can think of. It can be served as a side dish, like mashed potatoes (the two have a similar texture). This chapter contains a variety of polenta main dishes. After you learn the basics of this miraculous mush, you may substitute other ingredients and experiment to your heart's desire.

A note on cleanup: when washing up pots and utensils you have used to cook polenta, it is best to use cold water, which causes the polenta to lose its "cling."

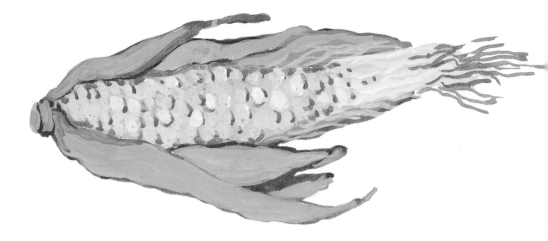

53
Basic Polenta
Polenta Tradizionale

This is the basic method for preparing perfect polenta. It takes time and attention, but as with everything good in life your patience and dedication will be rewarded. Alternatively, see the method for nontraditional polenta (*polenta realistica*), below.

Serves 4

4½ cups (1.1 L) water
1 teaspoon salt
1½ cups (266 g) polenta
1 tablespoon (14 g) unsalted butter or olive oil (optional)
¼ cup (43 g) grated Parmesan (optional)

Bring the water to a boil and add the salt. Lower the heat to medium and start adding the polenta in a very, very slow stream. (You might use a funnel, or place the polenta on a sheet of paper creased lengthwise.) Stir constantly with a whisk to minimize lumping. When you have added all the polenta, add the butter or olive oil if you are using them, mixing well. Lower the heat and cook for 30 minutes, stirring constantly and mashing out lumps as they form. The polenta will thicken, getting stiffer and drier as it cooks. Some traditionalists say that a wooden spoon will stand in it when it is done; others say that it will separate from the pot and come out as a clump. Mix in cheese before serving, if you wish.

If you are eating the polenta as is, serve immediately. Polenta continues to firm and thicken as it cools, so if you wish to shape it for further use, transfer it hot from the stove to whatever pan or form you are using.

Nontraditional Polenta: If you do not have the patience to pour the polenta into the boiling water one grain at a time or the 30 minutes to dedicate to stirring it and mashing lumps against the side of the pot, you can still enjoy polenta. Add the polenta to the boiling water as your time permits and when it lumps, as it inevitably will, have an eggbeater as well as a whisk handy (or, if you are a reckless iconoclast, an electric mixer) to smooth out the polenta. Or be philosophical: for earth people, lumps don't matter. As for cooking time, you can reduce it drastically, down to 10 or 15 minutes, or even less. You will notice some rawness in the polenta's taste and texture if you are eating it plain, but when it is cooked further with sauces and other ingredients, as in the following recipes, underdone, slightly lumpy, egg-beatered polenta will pass for "real" to all but the most discriminating palates.

Note: There are many "easy," no-lump methods for cooking polenta that involve mixing it with cold water and then bringing it to a boil, or mixing it with some cold water and adding the mixture to boiling water. These methods will insure smoothness but the result will not be the same as adding it dry to boiling water, especially in recipes which call for the polenta to be dried and recooked. Polenta prepared with cold water will not dry properly and sets very poorly.

54
Polenta-Tomato Pie
Polenta Torta con Pomodoro

There are several different ways to make a polenta pie. In this one, the polenta is formed into two layers, separated by cheese and a sauce and topped with the same. Make this recipe in a round 10-inch (25 cm), 2½-inch (6 cm)-deep cast-iron skillet. You will need another similar vessel to mold the top layer.

Serves 4

1 pound (454 g) fresh or canned tomatoes, peeled and chopped small (see page 13), 1 cup (237 mL) juice reserved

2 tablespoons (30 mL) olive oil

2 cloves garlic, pressed or minced

Salt to taste

¼ teaspoon crushed red pepper flakes, or to taste

20 whole fresh basil leaves

¼ cup (5 g) loosely packed chopped Italian parsley leaves

1 teaspoon oregano

1 Basic Polenta recipe (page 84), with optional butter and grated Parmesan added

1 cup (237 mL) tomato juice

6 ounces (170 g) mozzarella, grated

Place the tomatoes, olive oil, garlic, salt, crushed red pepper, basil, parsley, and oregano in a bowl. Mix well and set aside while you get the polenta ready. Oil the bottom of your casserole or skillet as well as that of a similarly shaped receptacle and set aside.

Cook the polenta as directed on page 84, using the tomato juice diluted with 3½ cups (828 mL) water instead of plain water. When the polenta is cooked, spoon half of it into each oiled pan. Let sit in a cool place for at least 1 hour. The polenta should become dry and solid, able to be transferred in one piece.

Preheat the oven to 375°F (190°C/gas 5). Lay two thirds of the tomato mixture on top of the polenta in the dish you will eventually bake in, then sprinkle over two thirds of the mozzarella. Remove the other layer of polenta from its dish and place it on top of the sauce. Top with the remaining tomato mixture, followed by the rest of the mozzarella.

Bake for 30 minutes, uncovered. Remove from the oven and let stand for 15 minutes before slicing into wedges or squares and serving.

55

Baked Polenta with Mushrooms and Goat Cheese

Polenta con Fungi e Formaggio Chevrino

In this dish the polenta and the other ingredients are all mixed together to form a uniform pie. It tends to be a bit more moist and mushy than Polenta-Tomato Pie (page 86). It is better to use a slightly larger baking dish for this recipe: a 12-inch (30 cm) round cast-iron skillet or a 10 by 12-inch (25 by 30 cm) baking dish, lightly oiled.

Serves 4

1 ounce (28 g) dried porcini mushrooms (ceps)
1 pound (454 g) fresh mushrooms (use regular white mushrooms or shiitake, crimini, portabello, or chanterelle mushrooms, mixed or alone)
¼ cup (59 mL) olive oil
2 cloves garlic, pressed or minced
3½ cups (828 mL) Vegetable Broth (page 36) or water
Salt to taste
1½ cups (266 g) polenta
1 tablespoon (14 g) butter
¼ cup (5 g) loosely packed chopped Italian parsley
4 ounces (113 g) goat cheese

Soak the dried porcini mushrooms in 1 cup (237 mL) of warm water for 15 minutes while you wash and dry the fresh mushrooms and cut them into slices. Drain the porcinis, cut them into ½-inch (1 cm) pieces, and add to the fresh mushrooms. Reserve the soaking water to add to the polenta cooking water.

Place olive oil in the pot you will eventually cook the polenta in and gently sauté garlic and mushrooms over medium-high heat until mushrooms are well coated with oil, infused with garlic, reduced in volume, and just beginning to soften, about 4 minutes. Set aside.

Without washing the pot, add to it the reserved porcini soaking water and 3½ cups (828 mL) of water or vegetable broth (you should have 4½ cups/1.1 L of liquid altogether) and bring to a boil. Add salt. Cook the polenta by traditional or untraditional method (see page 84), adding the butter at the beginning and the parsley and goat cheese at the end of cooking. Stir well until the cheese melts. Mix in the mushrooms and immediately transfer to the baking dish. Let polenta sit until it is cool and dry before baking, at least 1 hour.

Preheat the oven to 375°F (190°C/gas 5). Bake polenta uncovered for 30 minutes until top is brown. Remove from oven and let sit for 15 minutes before cutting it into squares or wedges and serving.

56

Polenta-Zucchini Casserole
Casserola di Polenta e Zucchini

This recipe is very simple. Instead of boiling, cooling, and
baking the polenta, as in the preceding two recipes, you
simply bake it. Use a 10-inch (25 cm) round cast-iron skillet
or an equivalent deep glass baking dish.
Peeling the zucchini (courgettes) is optional. Unpeeled, they
stay slightly firm and give the dish a greener look and more
character. Peeled, they melt into the polenta, forming with it
a more perfect union and firmer pie. If in doubt about how
you like it, peel half.

Serves 4

2 pounds (907 g) zucchini (courgettes)

¼ cup (59 mL) olive oil

8 ounces (227 g) mozzarella, grated or thinly sliced

6 tablespoons (59 g) finely minced onion

1½ cups (266 g) polenta

2 pounds (907 g) fresh or canned tomatoes, peeled and
  sliced (see page 13)

1 teaspoon oregano

Salt to taste

Crushed red pepper flakes to taste

Preheat the oven to 400°F (200°C/gas 6).

Wash the zucchini. Peel them if you like and cut them into thin rounds,
¼ inch (.6 cm) or less. Oil the bottom and sides of the baking dish with
1 tablespoon (15 mL) of olive oil. Place one third of the zucchini slices
in the baking dish. Place one third of the mozzarella on top of them, then
one third of the minced onions, followed by one third of the polenta, and
one third of the tomato slices. Drizzle over a tablespoon of olive oil, and
season with oregano, salt, and crushed red pepper.

Repeat for three layers. Make sure the top layer of polenta is well
covered with tomatoes so it will cook in their juices. If it seems too ex-
posed, moisten it with a tablespoon or two of water or, if you are using
canned tomatoes, the drained tomato juice. Bake uncovered for 1 hour.
Remove from oven and let sit for 15 minutes. Serve polenta in neat
wedges or squares.

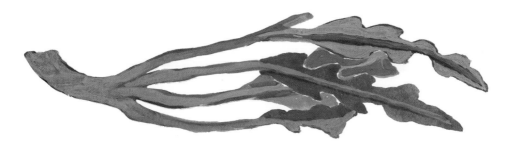

57
Grilled Polenta with White Beans and Arugula
Polenta Griglia con Cannellini e Rucola

These little cornmeal squares are very good as they are, but
even better with a topping. As with pizza, almost anything
will work, but I urge you to try them this way. You may use
spinach instead of arugula (rocket).

Serves 4

Basic Polenta (page 84)
1 large bunch arugula (rocket)
3 tablespoons (44 mL) olive oil
2 cloves garlic, pressed or minced
¼ teaspoon crushed red pepper flakes, or to taste
½ teaspoon oregano
Juice of ½ lemon
1 cup (170 g) canned cannellini beans, drained
4 ounces (113 g) mozzarella, grated

Cook the polenta by traditional or nontraditional method (see page
84). When it is cooked, spread it out to cool on a well-oiled baking sheet.
It should be about ½ inch (1 cm) thick.

Meanwhile, remove the lower stems from the arugula and wash, dry,
and chop it. Heat 2 tablespoons (30 mL) of the olive oil in a pot along
with the garlic and crushed red pepper. When the oil is hot add the arugula and quickly stir-fry. Add the oregano, lemon juice, and beans and
set aside.

When the polenta has cooled for at least 1 hour and can be handled
without falling apart, cut it into 4-inch (10 cm) squares. Turn the squares
over on the baking sheet so both sides are lightly oiled and place under
a hot broiler (grill) until browned, about 5 minutes for each side. Remove
from the oven and top each square with some of the cooked arugula and
bean mixture. Add mozzarella cheese and a drizzle of oil and return to
the broiler for a minute or two to melt the cheese. Serve hot.

58

Fried Polenta with Sundried Tomato and Olives
Polenta Fritta con Pomodoro Secco e Olive

Like grilled polenta, fried polenta can be served in a variety
of ways. Here is a recipe for one of the earthiest cornmeal
dishes under the sun.

Serves 4

Basic Polenta (page 84)

Sundried Tomato and Olive Pesto (page 50)

**Olive oil for frying, enough to come to ¼ inch (.6 cm) deep
in the pan**

Cook the polenta by traditional or nontraditional method (see page
84). When it is cooked, spread it out to cool on a lightly oiled board or
baking sheet. It should be about ½ inch (1 cm) thick.

Meanwhile, prepare the pesto.

When the polenta has cooled for at least 1 hour and can be handled
without falling apart, cut it into 4-inch (10 cm) squares. Fry squares in
hot olive oil until they are crusty and deep golden brown on both sides,
about 2 minutes per side.

Drain polenta squares on paper towels and serve with the pesto on the
side or spooned on top of each square.

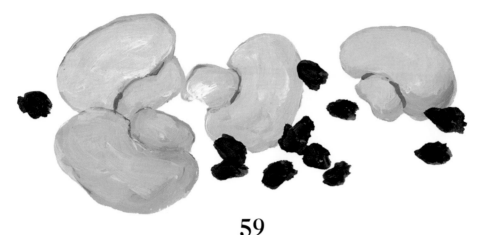

59
Creamy Polenta
Polenta Liscia

It is indeed possible to cook polenta by placing it in cold
water. Some traditionalists gasp in horror but this method
gives it a creamier texture, like porridge rather than mashed
potatoes. Prepared this way, polenta with raisins (sultanas),
honey, and nuts added makes a good breakfast cereal. Or add
sautéed mushrooms and garlic and serve as a side dish.

Serves 4

3 cups (710 mL) cold water
Salt to taste
1 cup (177 g) polenta
1 tablespoon (14 g) unsalted butter

Optional Ingredients
1 tablespoon (15 mL) honey
¼ cup (46 g) pine nuts
¼ cup (36 g) raisins (sultanas) or currants

or

¼ cup (43 g) grated Parmesan
1 cup (198 g) chopped mushrooms sautéed in oil and garlic

Place the water and salt in a pot. Add the polenta, stirring constantly
with a wooden spoon and bring to a boil. When it just starts to boil (be
careful! the first bubbles may burst with a splatter) lower the heat and
add the butter. Cover and cook as your patience and taste dictates, between 10 and 30 minutes. Add optional ingredients and let sit for 5 minutes, covered, over low heat. Serve hot.

VI
Pizzas
Pizze

Everyone loves pizza, especially when it's homemade and hot from the oven. Making a pie from scratch is more fun than getting a take-out pie, and need not be especially time-consuming. Other big advantages of making it yourself are that you have more options and that you can see that everything going into and onto the pizza is fresh and wholesome.

The basic pizza dough can be eaten with numerous ingredients. The toppings and stuffings in the recipes below are suggestions meant to whet the imagination as well as the appetite. Pizza is a canvas that allows you to mix and contrast different sauces, pestos, cheeses, and vegetables. Use whatever you like or whatever you have in your refrigerator or cupboard. If pineapple is your passion, do it!

There are various types of pizza—deep-dish, thin crust, stuffed, and so on. The same dough will work for most of them. This dough can be made using either unbleached all-purpose (plain) flour or semolina flour (the same flour that's used for pasta). The word *semolina* is derived from *semola*, the Italian for bran. Semolina consists of the gritty, coarse particles of wheat left after the finer flour has passed through the bolting (sifting) machine. Semolina dough has a rich amber color, firm texture, and a wheatier taste than the softer all-purpose flour.

Some home bakers prefer substituting whole wheat flour or cornmeal for 1 cup (184 g) of the all-purpose flour in pizza dough. The whole wheat makes the pizza crust nuttier and chewier, while the cornmeal makes it crunchy. You must be a little more careful when handling doughs made with whole wheat or cornmeal, as they tear easily. It is best to start your pizza-making career using ordinary unbleached all-purpose flour or semolina, or a combination of the two, and experiment later.

Ideally, for a crisp, delicious crust, pizza is baked on a hot stone or tile in a brick oven. The heat applied directly to the crust makes it crisp. The right equipment, such as pizza stones (either tiles or pieces of volcanic rock) and peels (long-handled shovel-like tools used to move the pies in and out of the oven), is helpful in making a great crust, but is by no means essential in making excellent pizza. While cast-iron grills and skillets work much better than aluminum baking sheets or glass baking dishes, a pie made in a disposable aluminum pan in an ordinary kitchen oven can still be delicious and leave nothing to be desired. A rolling-wheel knife gives you the satisfaction of spinning your creation into wedges, but a sharp serrated-edge knife will do as well. Likewise, a heavy-duty electric mixer or food processor with a dough hook makes mixing and kneading easier, but 10 minutes of pushing dough around with your palms and the heels of your hand works as well and allows you to put some of yourself into the dough.

Beginners should not worry too much about equipment. It's better to get the basics of making the dough under your belt first. If you have a large bowl, a flat pan, and a sharp knife, you're ready to make pizza.

The following recipes do not assume you own any bakery equipment. However, if you use a peel and an oven stone or tile, you do not need to oil these surfaces so the dough won't stick: a little cornmeal dusted on the peel is sufficient. Other cooking surfaces, such as skillets or baking sheets, should be lightly oiled and sprinkled with cornmeal before the pie is set on them.

Basic Pizza Dough

It's as easy as pie!
To make the dough, you need about 1 cup (237 mL) of water
for every 3 cups (710 mL) of flour. You may need more water
to make a dough you can easily knead, especially if you are
using semolina flour, which absorbs more water than all-
purpose (plain) flour. To get the yeast working, dissolve it is
lukewarm water (about 110°F/43°C); the water should feel
fairly warm to your hand but not hot. The dough should rise
in a place that is at least 75°F (23°C).

Makes 2 12-inch pizzas

1 teaspoon (7 g) sugar
2 teaspoons (¼ ounce/7 g/1 package) active dry yeast
1 cup (237 mL) warm water
1 teaspoon (7 g) salt
2 tablespoons (30 mL) olive oil
3 cups (553 g) unbleached all-purpose (plain) flour, semolina
flour, or a combination, plus some extra for handling

In a bowl large enough to accommodate the flour, mix the sugar and
the yeast together. Add half the water and stir with a wooden spoon to
dissolve the yeast and sugar. Let stand for 5 to 10 minutes, until the yeast
begins to foam. Stir in the olive oil and the salt. Add the flour and mix.
Add the remaining warm water a little at a time until you have a ball of
dough. If it is too runny, add more flour; if it is too stiff, add more water.
Working with your hands, knead the dough for 5 to 10 minutes, either in
a bowl or on a floured work surface, until it is smooth, slightly moist, and
elastic. If using a mixer with a blade or dough hook, put the flour, olive
oil, salt, yeast, and sugar mixture in the bowl and process for about 2
minutes, adding the remaining water a little at a time through the feed
tube, until the dough pulls away from the side of the bowl. (If the dough
continues to stick, add more flour a little at a time.) Coat the entire surface of the dough ball with a small amount of olive oil and return the
dough to the bowl (in the case of Sicilian Pizza [page 97] and the Thin
Crust Round Pizzas [page 98], you may put the dough directly into the
baking dish you will use and let it rise there). Cover the bowl with a
clean, damp towel, and let sit in a warm place for an hour or two, until it
has doubled in size. Then proceed with the recipe.

60
Sicilian Pizza
Pizza alla Siciliano

From the mountains of Sicily to Eighteenth Avenue in Brooklyn, Sicilians like their pizza crust thick and their pies square. Forming the dough inside the pan saves time and mess; use a rectangular pan, 10 by 13 inches (25 by 33 cm).

Makes 1 pizza: serves 4 to 6

Basic Pizza Dough (page 95)
5 tablespoons (74 mL) olive oil
1 onion, sliced thin
2 pounds (907 g) fresh or canned tomatoes, peeled and chopped (see page 13)
6 ounces (170 g) mozzarella, grated
1 teaspoon oregano
¼ teaspoon crushed red pepper flakes, or to taste

After forming the dough, oil the bottom and sides of the pan, sprinkle a little cornmeal, place the ball in the pan, press it out until it fills the pan and is evenly distributed, and allow to rise. Put 2 tablespoons (30 mL) of the olive oil in a pan and sauté the onion for 7 to 10 minutes over medium heat until they are thoroughly soft and transparent.

Meanwhile, preheat the oven to 425°F (220°C/gas 7).

Lay the onion slices on the dough, then spread the tomatoes in an even layer, then the cheese. Sprinkle the oregano and crushed red pepper over the top. Drizzle the remaining olive oil over everything. Place the pizza in the center of the oven and bake for 20 to 25 minutes, until the crust is browned and the cheese is melted and bubbling.

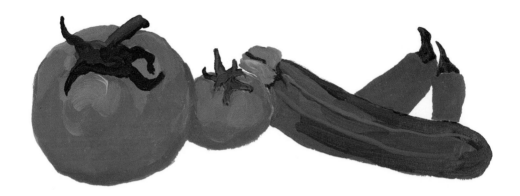

61
Thin Crust Round Pizza with Tomatoes and Basil
or Basil Pesto and Zucchini
Pizza alla Napoletana

One recipe of basic dough is enough for two 12-inch (30 cm)
round pizzas. Topping suggests are for one pie each; you can
simply double either topping recipe if you want two pizzas
with the same topping, or, if you are making only one pizza,
you can refrigerate or freeze the other ball of dough. As in
the recipe for Sicilian Pizza (page 97), you can save yourself
the trouble and mess of rolling out the dough by allowing it
to rise in the pans.

Makes 2 pizzas: serves 4 to 6

Basic Pizza Dough (page 95)

Red Topping (Tomato and Basil)
2 pounds (907 g) fresh or canned tomatoes, peeled and
chopped small (see page 13)
20 whole fresh basil leaves
4 ounces (113 g) mozzarella, grated
Crushed red pepper flakes to taste
2 teaspoons oregano
2 tablespoons (30 mL) olive oil

Green Topping (Basil Pesto and Zucchini)
1 cup (237 mL) Basil Pesto (page 24)
4 ounces (113 g) mozzarella, grated
1 small zucchini (courgette), peeled and cut in thin rounds
1 tablespoon (15 mL) olive oil

If you have allowed the dough to rise in the baking pan, use your fingers to press it out to the edges of the pan. Otherwise, once the dough has risen, divide it into two balls and roll each one in a circle 12 inches (30 cm) in diameter. In either case, oil your pans or skillets and sprinkle them with a little cornmeal or flour before laying crusts on them.

Preheat the oven to 425°F (220°C/gas 7).

For the red topping, layer the tomatoes, basil, mozzarella cheese, crushed red pepper, and oregano in that order on one circle of pizza dough. Drizzle the olive oil on top.

For the green topping, spread the pesto uniformly over the other circle of dough. Top with the grated mozzarella. Toss the zucchini slices in the olive oil and lay them on the pizza.

Bake the pizzas for 15 to 20 minutes, until their crusts are browned and their cheese toppings are melted and bubbling.

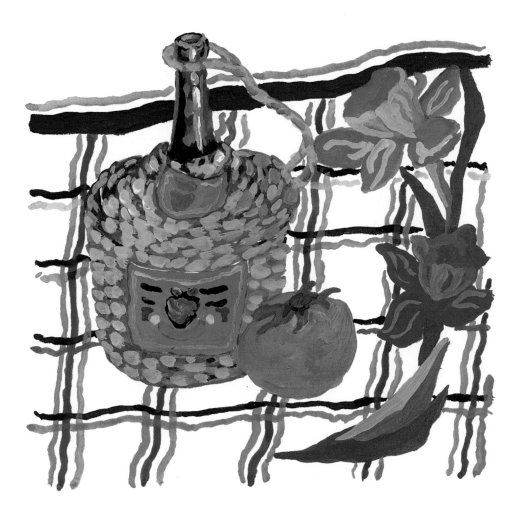

62
Pizza Rolls with Spinach, Herbs, and Cheese *or* Broccoli, Tomatoes, and Cheese
Pizza Involtini di Verdura e Formaggio

Depending on how you look at this dish, it is a kind of rolled pizza or stuffed bread. One basic pizza dough recipe will yield enough for two 12-inch (30 cm) rolls. There are two different fillings here, but you can simply double either one if you want two pizza rolls with the same filling. A half-hour before you're ready to roll, prepare the fillings. Vegetables should be at room temperature before they go onto the dough.

Makes 2 rolls: serves 4 to 6

Basic Pizza Dough (page 95)

Spinach and Herb Filling
2 tablespoons (30 mL) olive oil
¼ teaspoon crushed red pepper flakes, or to taste
10 ounces spinach, washed, dried, with stems removed, and chopped
¼ teaspoon nutmeg
¼ teaspoon rosemary
Salt to taste
4 ounces (113 g) mozzarella, grated

Broccoli and Tomato Filling
2 cups (347 g) small (1-inch/2.5 cm) broccoli florets
3 cloves garlic, pressed or minced
¼ teaspoon crushed red pepper flakes, or to taste
2 tablespoons (30 mL) olive oil
3 plum tomatoes, peeled and chopped (see page 13)
Salt to taste
8 ounces (227 g) ricotta
2 tablespoons (21 g) grated Parmesan

Prepare the dough and then the fillings; have the cheese on hand. Preheat the oven to 425°F (220°C/gas 7).

To make the spinach and herb filling, place the oil in a large, heavy pot over high heat. Add the crushed red pepper. When the oil is very hot but not burning, add the spinach, stirring it so it will wilt evenly.

Continue sautéing until the spinach is considerably reduced in bulk, about 3 minutes. Add the nutmeg, rosemary, and salt and stir well. Remove from heat and set aside to cool to room temperature.

To make the broccoli and tomato filling, boil the broccoli florets in 2 cups (473 mL) of water for a minute or two to soften them. Drain, saving the water for soup stock if you like. Heat the garlic and crushed red pepper in the oil over medium-high heat. Then add the broccoli and stir for 1 minute. Then add the tomatoes and salt and stir for another minute. Lower the heat, cover, and cook for 5 minutes, until the broccoli is thoroughly soft. Remove from heat and cool to room temperature.

Divide the risen dough in half. Place each half on a floured board and roll into a circle about 12 inches (30 cm) in diameter.

On one dough circle spread the spinach topping evenly, then sprinkle the mozzarella on top of it. On the other dough circle, spread the broccoli and tomato topping. (There might be some liquid from the tomatoes. Do not use it on the pizza. Rather, drain it off and add it to your stock to use another time.) Top with the ricotta and Parmesan.

Now carefully roll up the circles with the filling inside as tightly as you can without ripping the dough. Crimp the edges with your fingers. If some of the filling squeezes out at the ends, don't force it back in. Spread it on top; it will bake into the dough. The rolls should look something like 12-inch (30 cm) loaves of Italian bread.

Lightly oil a baking sheet and dust it with cornmeal or all-purpose flour. Bake until crusts are golden brown, about 25 to 30 minutes. Cut each roll into four 3-inch slices with a sharp knife. Serve warm. This dish can also be eaten the next day at room temperature.

63
Covered Pizza Stuffed with Broccoli and Mushrooms
Sfincione

"Covered" pizza is very Sicilian and is served everywhere in Palermo. The basic dough recipe will make one 12-inch (30 cm) pie. The addition of the cornmeal to the filling helps the pie stay firm by absorbing any extra liquid—when you cut it, you will want the filling to be firm. Vegetables must be at room temperature before going onto the dough, so leave enough time.
Assemble this pie on the pan, baking sheet, or skillet you will bake it in. Once filled, it will be difficult to move.

Makes 1 pizza: serves 4

Basic Pizza Dough (page 95)

Filling
1½ cups (298 g) small (1-inch/2.5 cm) broccoli florets
2 cloves garlic, pressed or minced
¼ teaspoon crushed red pepper flakes, or to taste
3 tablespoons (44 mL) olive oil
1½ cups (298 g) 1-inch (2.5) mushroom slices
Salt to taste
8 sundried tomatoes, packed in oil, chopped
¼ teaspoon grated nutmeg
8 ounces (227 g) ricotta
4 ounces (113 g) mozzarella
2 tablespoons (30 mL) grated Parmesan
2 tablespoons (22 g) cornmeal, plus extra for dusting the pan

Boil the broccoli florets in 2 cups (473 mL) of water for a minute or two to soften them. Drain, saving the water for soup stock if you like. Heat the garlic and crushed red pepper in the oil over medium-high heat. Add the broccoli and stir for 1 minute. Add the mushrooms and stir for another minute. Lower heat, cover, and cook for 3 minutes, until the broccoli is soft. Add the salt, sundried tomatoes, and nutmeg and stir. Remove from heat and set aside to cool to room temperature.

Preheat oven to 425°F (220°C/gas 7).

Mix the ricotta, mozzarella, and Parmesan together in a bowl. When the broccoli and mushroom mixture is cool, stir in the cheeses and the 2 tablespoons of cornmeal.

Cut the dough in two, one part slightly larger than the other. Roll into two circles, one 13 inches (33 cm) in diameter and the other 12 inches (30 cm) in diameter. Oil the pizza pan and dust it with cornmeal. Place the larger circle on the prepared pizza pan and turn the filling out onto it. Spread with a wooden spoon up to ½ inch (1 cm) from the edge of the dough. Put the smaller circle of dough on top and pinch the edges of the bottom and top together, using a little water on your fingers to make a better seal. Poke a small hole in the center to let steam escape.

Place the pie in the oven and bake for 25 to 30 minutes, until the crust is brown. Let sit for 5 minutes before slicing.

64
Calzone Filled with Eggplant and Cheese *or* Roasted Peppers and Cheese
Calzone

This recipe will make six main-dish–sized calzone. Often calzone are served with tomato sauce on top or on the side, so, if you like, whip up a batch of Basic Tomato Sauce to serve with these turnovers. Each filling recipe below will fill three calzone; feel free to double the quantities if you want only one kind of filling. For additional ideas for filling, see the recipe for Baking Soda–Crust Calzone (page 106).

Makes 6 calzone

Basic Pizza Dough (page 95)

Eggplant Filling
Salt
1 pound (454 g) eggplant (aubergine), cut into ½-inch (1 cm) cubes
2 tablespoons (30 mL) olive oil
4 ounces (113 g) mozzarella, grated
8 ounces (227 g) ricotta
2 tablespoons (21 g) grated Parmesan

Roasted Pepper Filling
2 pounds (907 g) bell peppers (capsicums), roasted and peeled (see page 25)
1 teaspoon oregano
2 teaspoons (10 mL) olive oil
4 ounces (113 g) mozzarella, grated
4 ounces (113 g) goat cheese, crumbled

Basic Tomato Sauce (page 48) (optional)

To make the eggplant filling, salt the eggplant cubes and leave them to drain for 30 minutes. Gently squeeze out excess liquid. Heat the olive oil over medium heat and fry the eggplant until it is very soft, about 5 minutes. Remove from heat, cool to room temperature, then add cheeses.

To make the roasted pepper filling, cut the peppers into 1-inch (2.5 cm) strips and toss them with the oregano and olive oil. Make sure filling is at room temperature before you add the cheeses.

Preheat oven to 425°F (220°C/gas 7).

Cut the dough into 6 even pieces and form each piece into a ball. On a floured work surface, roll each ball into an 8-inch (20 cm) circle. Place equal amounts of the fillings on one side of each circle and fold over into half-moon shaped dumplings. Do not overfill. Wet the edges with a little water and seal them with a fork or your fingers. Place the calzone on an oiled baking sheet that has been dusted with cornmeal and bake for 20 to 25 minutes until their tops are crusty and slightly browned. Serve with tomato sauce, if you like.

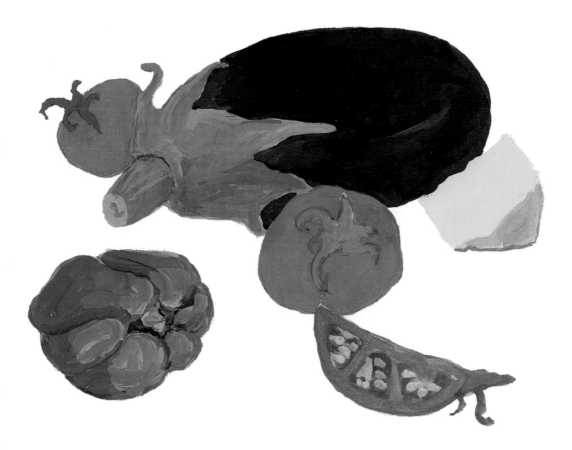

65
Baking Soda–Crust Calzone with Olives, Tomatoes, and Four Cheeses
Calzone Pronti

Here is a way to turn any combination of ingredients or
leftovers into a quick and unique meal. Use the suggested
fillings, or improvise your own; you should have about 3 cups
(710 mL) of filling. This dough is not as elastic as yeast
dough, so be careful not to break it.
As with the yeast calzones, these can be fried or baked.
They will take about 20 to 25 minutes in a 425°F (220°C/gas
7) oven. If you are frying them, you may be able to put these
on the table in under 15 minutes.

Makes 6 calzone: serves 6 as a main dish

Filling
2 pounds (907 g) plum tomatoes, peeled and chopped (see
page 13)
2 tablespoons (22 g) cornmeal
8 ounces (227 g) ricotta
4 ounces (113 g) provolone, grated
¼ cup (43 g) grated Parmesan
8 black olives, pitted and chopped
6 sundried tomatoes packed in oil, chopped
1 onion, chopped and sautéed in olive oil
10 fresh basil leaves, chopped

Dough
3 cups (552 g) unbleached all-purpose (plain) flour
1 tablespoon (15 g) baking powder
1 teaspoon (7 g) salt
About 1 cup (237 mL) lukewarm water

Oil for frying (olive oil mixed equally with soybean or corn
oil, enough to come to a generous ¼ inch (.6 cm) deep in
the pan) (optional)
Basic Tomato Sauce (page 28) (optional)

Mix filling ingredients together and set aside.

To make the dough, mix the flour, baking powder, and salt together. Add water a little at a time, mixing with a wooden spoon until you have formed a firm, elastic dough. (No need to knead.) Cut the dough ball into 6 even pieces and form each piece into a ball. On a floured work surface, roll each ball into an 8-inch (20 cm) circle. Place equal amounts of filling on one side of each circle and fold over to make half-moon–shaped dumplings. Do not overfill. Wet the edges with a little water and seal them with a fork or your fingers.

If you are frying the calzone, heat the oil in a skillet (at least 10 inches/ 25 cm in diameter). When the oil is very hot gently slip in one calzone. You may be able to fit two at a time into a 12-inch (30 cm) skillet. Do not crowd them. Fry calzone for 1 or 2 minutes on one side, until the dough rises and turns brown. Gently turn over and cook for another minute or so on the other side. Remove from the oil and drain on paper towels or brown paper. Continue until all calzone are fried.

If you are baking the calzone, preheat the oven to 425°F (220°C/gas 7). Place the calzone gently on an oiled baking sheet that has been dusted with cornmeal, and bake for 20 to 25 minutes, until their tops are crusty and slightly browned. These calzone should sit a minute or two before serving. They can be served with tomato sauce on top or on the side.

66
Tomato Pizza Bread with Rosemary and Olives
Focacce

This thick-crust round pizza has a dimpled surface with olives, rosemary, and tomatoes baked into it. It is drier than most pizza and is best served with extra virgin olive oil as an antipasto. When you are preparing the dough, knead the rosemary into it. It is also very good with 1 cup (184 g) of cornmeal substituted for 1 cup of the flour in the basic dough recipe.

> Basic Pizza Dough (page 95), adding 2 tablespoons fresh rosemary or 1 tablespoon dried
>
> ⅓ cup (47 g) pitted and coarsely chopped green olives, packed in oil
>
> 1 pound (454 g) fresh or canned tomatoes, peeled and chopped (see page 13)
>
> 8 sundried tomatoes, packed in oil, chopped
>
> ½ cup (86 g) coarsely grated Parmesan
>
> 2 tablespoons (30 mL) extra virgin olive oil, plus additional to serve

Preheat oven to 425°F (220°C/gas 7).

Oil a 10-inch (25 cm) cast-iron skillet and sprinkle with cornmeal. Press the dough out evenly in the oiled skillet. Dimple the surface of the dough and press the olives, chopped tomatoes, and sundried tomatoes into the dough. Top with the Parmesan and drizzle with the 2 tablespoons olive oil. Bake 20 to 25 minutes, until top is well browned.

This bread can be eaten hot from the oven or at room temperature, with olive oil or not.

VII
Eggs
Uova

Eggs may not be strictly vegetarian, but neither are they meat. Any way you look at them, they are both an excellent source of protein and a marvelous setting for vegetables—especially in the classic Italian egg dish, the frittata.

The frittata (or *frocia* as it is sometimes called in Sicily) is an Italian omelet, an egg pie cooked slowly over low heat. Frittatas should be firm, not runny, and light yellow or golden, never burnt or brown. They can be eaten plain or as filling in a sandwich. Have them for breakfast or lunch, as an antipasto or a light supper. They are usually cut into pie-shaped wedges and can be served hot, cold, or at room temperature.

The amounts of butter and oil used in the frittata recipes are gauged for a seasoned 10-inch (25 cm) round cast-iron skillet with a tight-fitting lid. Sicilians would typically use 2 tablespoons (30 mL) of olive oil, while Americans, used to buttery omelets, would use 2 tablespoons (28 g) of butter (or more). In line with the best-of-both-worlds philosophy, the recipes for frittatas in this book call for 1 tablespoon (14 g) of butter and 1 tablespoon (15 mL) of olive

oil. You may adjust according to your taste, but be careful when heating the butter not to burn it.

Pans with artificial nonstick surfaces will allow you to reduce the amounts of oil and butter. (You might have to increase the fat a bit for an unseasoned cast-iron pan or decrease it if you have a very well-seasoned cast-iron or cast-iron enamel pan.) Pans without plastic parts (which includes nonstick surfaces) can spare you the ordeal of flipping the frittata by allowing you, once the bottom of the frittata has set, to place it briefly under the broiler to cook the top. Otherwise, you must transfer it to a plate, with the set side down, then turn it over onto the pan. Only cooks with out-of-hand *Sicilianismo* would dare flip an egg pie in the air like a flapjack.

The cooking time for frittatas varies with the ingredients and your conception of what "low heat" means. The lower the heat the better. A Tomato, Basil, and Cheese Frittata (page 115), in which raw ingredients are added to the eggs, is going to take longer than one such as Pepper Frittata (page 113) in which the eggs are poured over already-cooked vegetables. While the omelet is cooking it might seem to be sticking to the pan. Have faith; do not poke at it. As it cooks it will come off the bottom of the pan. When you think it is done on the bottom, shake the pan and do a little gentle prodding. If the frittata is loose and moves as a piece, it is ready for flipping or the broiler.

Frittatas can be made using almost any herb or vegetable. In the following recipes, variations are given.

67
Parsley Frittata
Frittata di Prezzemolo

This is a simple frittata to start with. Use only the leaves of
the parsley for this recipe. They should be fresh—crisp,
deep green, and sweet. You can also mix chives, tarragon,
thyme, or basil with the parsley.

Serves 4

6 eggs
Salt to taste
¼ teaspoon crushed red pepper flakes, or to taste
2 cups (43 g) loosely packed chopped Italian parsley leaves
1 tablespoon (14 g) butter
1 tablespoon (15 mL) olive oil
2 ounces (57 g) mozzarella, grated

Break the eggs into a bowl. Add the salt and crushed red pepper. Beat
until eggs are foamy. Mix in the parsley and beat some more.

Heat the butter and the olive oil in a 10-inch (25 cm) skillet with a
tight-fitting lid over very low heat. When the butter has melted, add the
egg mixture, tilting the pan from side to side to spread the eggs evenly.
Sprinkle the cheese uniformly on top. Cover the pan and cook until the
bottom is set, about 15 or 20 minutes. Then cook the top, either by
placing the frittata under the broiler for a few minutes, or by transferring
it to a plate and turning it back into the skillet and cooking for about 3
minutes, until the egg sets. When done, cut into wedges and serve hot,
cold, or at room temperature.

68
Pepper Frittata
Frittata di Peperoni

Try this on warm semolina bread for the greatest egg
sandwich ever. For a hot pepper omelet, dice a jalapeño chile
and add it to the pan with the scallions. For a zucchini
(courgette) pie, leave out the roasted peppers and substitute
1 pound (454 g) peeled raw zucchini cut
into ½-inch (1 cm) cubes.

Serves 4

1 small potato

1 pound (454 g) green or red bell peppers (capsicum),
   roasted (see page 25)

1 tablespoon (14 g) butter

1 tablespoon (15 mL) oil

6 scallions (spring onions), chopped small

6 eggs

¼ cup (5 g) loosely packed Italian parsley leaves

2 tablespoons (21 g) grated Parmesan

Salt to taste

¼ teaspoon crushed red pepper flakes, or to taste

Peel and quarter the potato, then chop it into ½-inch (1 cm) cubes.
Boil for 2 minutes, drain, and set aside. Cut the roasted peppers into ½-
inch (1 cm) squares and set aside.

In a 10-inch (25 cm) skillet with a tight-fitting lid, melt the butter in
the oil over medium heat. Add the chopped scallions and sauté for 3
minutes, stirring. Add the potato cubes and sauté for 2 minutes. Add the
peppers and sauté for another 2 minutes. Lower heat, cover, and simmer
for 10 minutes until vegetables are soft.

Beat the eggs until they are foamy. Add the parsley, cheese, salt, and
crushed red pepper, and beat some more. Spread the vegetables evenly
over the bottom of the skillet and pour in the egg mixture. Cover the pan
and cook for about 15 or 20 minutes over very low heat. Then cook the
top, either by placing the frittata under the broiler for a few minutes or
by transferring it to a plate and turning it back into the skillet and cooking
for about 3 minutes, until the egg sets. When done, cut into wedges and
serve hot, cold, or at room temperature.

69
Broccoli Frittata
Frittata di Broccoli

This recipe is for garlic lovers as well as broccoli aficionados.
You may also try asparagus spears, cut into 1-inch (2.5 cm)
lengths, in place of the broccoli.

2 cups (397 g) small (1-inch/2.5 cm) broccoli florets
6 cloves garlic, sliced thin
1 tablespoon (15 mL) olive oil
1 tablespoon (14 g) butter
6 eggs
Salt to taste
¼ teaspoon crushed red pepper flakes, or to taste
½ cup (85 g) grated Parmesan

Boil the broccoli florets in 2 cups (473 mL) of water for 2 or 3 minutes.
Drain well, saving the water for soup stock if you like. In a 10-inch (25
cm) skillet with a tight-fitting lid, sauté the garlic over medium heat in
the olive oil and the butter until almost golden. Add the broccoli and stir-
fir a few minutes until broccoli is coated with oil. Lower heat, cover, and
cook until the broccoli is tender, about 10 minutes. Add a tablespoon (15
mL) of the cooking water if it seems to dry.

In a bowl, beat the eggs with the salt and crushed red pepper until
eggs are foamy.

Distribute the broccoli evenly in the skillet and pour the beaten eggs
over it. Sprinkle the cheese uniformly on top. Cover and cook over very
low heat until eggs are set on the bottom, about 15 or 20 minutes. Then
cook the top, either by placing the frittata under the broiler for a few
minutes, or by transferring it to a plate and turning it back into the skillet
and cooking for about 3 minutes, until the egg sets. When done, cut into
wedges and serve hot, cold, or at room temperature.

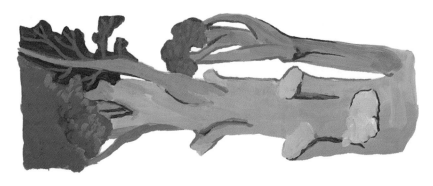

70
Tomato, Basil, and Cheese Frittata
Frittata Caprese

Use fresh basil for this recipe. If using canned tomatoes,
remember to drain them well, both before and after
chopping. For a creamy omelet use well-crumbled goat
cheese—Montrachet, or *bûcheron*—or for a more Italian taste,
use fresh mozzarella.

Serves 4

6 eggs
Salt to taste
¼ teaspoon crushed red pepper flakes, or to taste
1 tablespoon (14 g) butter
2 tablespoons (30 mL) olive oil
1 pound (454 g) tomatoes, peeled and chopped (see page 13)
20 large basil leaves, julienned
4 ounces (113 g) cheese, either crumbled goat cheese or
    grated or chopped mozzarella

In a large bowl beat the eggs with the salt and crushed red pepper until
the eggs are foamy.

Melt the butter in the olive oil over low heat in a 10-inch (25 cm) skillet
with a tight-fitting lid. Add the beaten eggs, tilting the pan if necessary
to distribute the eggs evenly. Add the tomatoes, then the basil, then the
cheese, distributing evenly. Cover the pan and cook over very low heat
for 30 minutes, or until the bottom of the eggs is set. Then cook the top,
either by placing the frittata under the broiler for a few minutes, or by
transferring it to a plate and turning it back into the skillet and cooking
for about 3 minutes, until the egg sets. When done, cut into wedges and
serve hot, cold, or at room temperature.

71
Mayonnaise
Salsa Maionese

Legend has it that Sicilian-born chef Amelio Butero, who
worked in the service of the Duke of Richelieu, invented
and named this dressing in honor of his Grace's capture of
the city of Mahón, the capital of Minorca, in 1756. Whatever
its origins, mayonnaise is a Mediterranean dish. Homemade
is far superior to store-bought, and surprisingly easy to make
if you have a blender.
For a fresher taste, use lemon juice; if you like a spread with
some character, use a good quality wine vinegar. Use extra
virgin olive oil. Finely minced garlic or other herbs can be
added with the oil to make a tasty dressing for hard-boiled
eggs or vegetables. Since you will be eating raw yolk, it's
best to use farm-fresh eggs from free-range chickens.
Mayonnaise will keep in the refrigerator for 2 or 3 days.

Makes 1 cup

2 egg yolks
Salt and black pepper to taste
3 tablespoons (44 mL) lemon juice or white wine vinegar
1 cup (237 mL) olive oil

Place egg yolks, salt and pepper, and lemon juice or vinegar in a
blender or food processor and blend on medium speed until the yolks
are creamy. Drizzle in the oil SLOWLY as you continue blending. Stop
when the mayonnaise has thickened and is stiff, not runny.

72
Sicilian Egg Salad
Insalata Uova

This is great on toast. Here is one instance where brine-packed bottled green olives work better than the heavily seasoned oil-packed ones. This egg salad is good "deviled" with plenty of hot pepper, but go easy on the salt, as the olives add plenty. The finer you chop the vegetables the better, so take your time. This salad has a wonderful spreadable quality when the vegetables are well minced.

Serves 4

40 pitted green olives (with or without pimiento), bottled in brine

6 eggs

3 stalks celery, washed, dried, and ends trimmed

3 scallions (spring onions), ends trimmed, outer skins removed

½ cup (10 g) loosely packed Italian parsley leaves

½ green bell pepper (capsicum)

½ red bell pepper (capsicum), roasted (see page 25)

Sliced fresh hot chile pepper, crushed red pepper flakes, or cayenne pepper to taste

¼ cup (59 mL) mayonnaise (page 116), or more to taste

Drain and dry the olives and set them aside to cool.

Place the eggs in lukewarm water, bring to boil over medium heat, and boil for about 10 minutes. Remove them from the heat, drain, run them under cool water to stop them cooking, and set aside to cool.

Place all remaining ingredients, including the olives but not the mayonnaise, on a large chopping board, and chop with a good knife for about 10 minutes, until everything is evenly and very finely chopped. Place chopped ingredients in a large bowl.

Remove the eggs from their shells and chop them small. (You needn't be as meticulous as with the vegetables; the eggs will crumble when you mix the salad.) Add the eggs to the bowl with the vegetable mixture and toss well.

Add mayonnaise a little at a time, mixing it in with two forks. The salad should be *lightly* dressed so the colors of the vegetables come through, but you should be able to scrape it from the sides of the bowl with a spatula and form it into a cohesive ball. Serve with toast and additional mayonnaise, if desired.

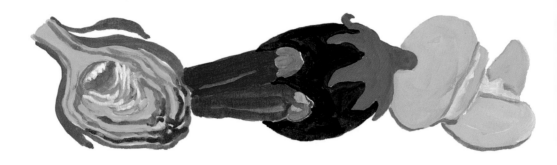

VIII
Specialties
Piatti Speciali

Every restaurant in Sicily, every family, and every cook of Sicilian descent has his or her specialties. Stuffed vegetables are typical of Sicilian cooking, and there are dozens of ways of filling hollowed zucchini (courgettes), eggplant (aubergines), bell peppers (capsicums), tomatoes, cabbage, artichokes, mushrooms, and so forth; using rice, pasta, cornmeal, bread crumbs, herbs and flavorings, and even vegetables. A sampling of stuffed dishes is offered here, along with other miscellaneous specialties, including Eggplant Parmesan, Eggplant Rolls, and several versions of fried and grilled vegetables—of which there are hundreds of other variations.

73
Stuffed Zucchini
Barzini

Barzini means boats, and even loaded with filling, these hollowed-out zucchini (courgettes) look as if they will float. This stuffing is flavored with savory porcini mushrooms (ceps). A medium zucchini is one that weighs about ½ pound (227 g). Larger zucchini have more water and less flavor; however, if fresh, a single titanic squash can be used here with satisfying, even impressive, results.

Serves 4

1 ounce (28 g) dried porcini mushrooms (ceps)
½ pound (227 g) fresh or canned tomatoes, peeled and
    chopped (see page 13)
4 zucchini (courgettes), about 2 pounds (907 g) total weight
¼ cup (59 mL) olive oil
¼ teaspoon crushed red pepper flakes, or to taste
½ cup (78 g) finely minced onion (about ½ an onion)
1 clove garlic, crushed or finely minced
Salt to taste
½ teaspoon oregano
1 cup (128 g) unseasoned dried bread crumbs (see page 28)
½ cup (86 g) Parmesan, pecorino, or locatelli cheese, grated
2 tablespoons white wine (optional)

Break or cut porcini mushrooms into small pieces. Combine with the tomatoes and set aside.

Wash zucchini but do not peel. Cut in half lengthwise. Scoop out centers, then scrape out the flesh near the skins, leaving ¼-inch (.6 cm) shells. Rub the shells inside and out with about 1 tablespoon (15 mL) of the olive oil and set aside. Chop scooped out and scraped zucchini finely and set aside.

Preheat oven to 375°F (190°C/gas 5).

Heat the remaining olive oil in a large skillet. Add crushed red pepper, onion, and garlic. Sauté over medium heat until onion softens, about 5 minutes. Raise the heat and add the chopped, scooped out zucchini. Sauté 1 minute, stirring all the while, so it is slightly reduced. Add the mushrooms and tomatoes, salt, and oregano and sauté, stirring, for 1 more minute. Remove from heat. Add the bread crumbs and cheese and mix thoroughly. The mixture should form a stiff stuffing that you can mold with your hands. If the mixture seems too wet, add more bread crumbs; if too dry, add a tablespoon or two or white wine. Load the stuffing into the prepared zucchini hulls.

Arrange the boats on an oiled baking dish. Bake 30 minutes or until zucchini is soft and stuffing is brown.

74
Eggplant Rolls
Melanzane Involtini

In the domain of Sicilian meatless main dishes, eggplant (aubergine) is king. Like eggplant *parmigiana*, these rolls are great served with bread and a salad. They are a lot of work, but they're worth it.

Makes 12 rolls: serves 4 to 6

2 medium eggplants (aubergines), about 2 pounds (907 g) total weight

Salt

10 ounces (283 g) spinach

½ teaspoon crushed red pepper flakes, or to taste

½ cup (118 mL) olive oil

¼ teaspoon dried rosemary

¼ teaspoon nutmeg

1 cup (184 g) unbleached all-purpose (plain) flour

1 cup (128 g) unseasoned dried bread crumbs (see page 28)

2 eggs

2 cloves garlic, pressed or finely minced

2 pounds (907 g) tomatoes, peeled, and chopped (see page 13)

12 large whole basil leaves or 1 teaspoon dried basil

½ teaspoon dried oregano

8 ounces (227 g) ricotta

4 ounces (113 g) mozzarella, grated

¼ cup (43 g) grated Parmesan

Peel the eggplants and slice each lengthwise into six ½-inch (1 cm) slices. Salt slices and let them sit to drain for 30 minutes in a colander.

Meanwhile, remove the stems from the spinach, wash and dry the leaves, and chop them small. Heat ¼ teaspoon of the crushed red pepper in 2 tablespoons (30 mL) of the olive oil in a pan over high heat and add the chopped spinach. Cook, stirring constantly, until the spinach is very soft, about 3 or 4 minutes. Stir in rosemary and nutmeg, remove from heat, and allow to cool.

Preheat the oven to 400°F (200°C/gas 6).

Mix the flour and the bread crumbs together. In a separate bowl, beat the eggs and set aside. Gently squeeze the eggplant slices to drain excess moisture, and wipe off any remaining salt. Dip the eggplant slices into the eggs, then coat entirely with the flour and bread crumb mixture.

Pour 2 tablespoons (30 mL) of the olive oil into a large baking dish or dishes. (If you have to use two dishes, you might need a bit more oil.) Place the eggplant in the pans; the slices should not overlap. Sprinkle tops with 2 tablespoons of the olive oil. Then place the dish or dishes in the oven until the eggplant slices are brown, about 30 minutes, turning once after 20 minutes.

Meanwhile, put the remaining 2 tablespoons of olive oil in a pan. Add ¼ teaspoon of crushed red pepper and the garlic and sauté over high heat until they sizzle. Add the tomatoes, basil, and oregano and cook over low heat, covered, for 20 minutes.

Add ricotta, mozzarella, and grated Parmesan to the now-cooled spinach and mix well. When the eggplant is cooked, remove it from the oven and place a tablespoon or two of the cheese-spinach mixture in a line lengthwise down the center of each slice. Fold the slices up lengthwise over the cheese and spinach, like hot dog rolls. Arrange in a smaller baking dish and gently spoon tomato sauce over each one. Bake at 350°F (180°C/gas 4) for ½ hour. Serve hot or at room temperature with Italian bread and a simple green salad.

75
Baked Whole Zucchini
Zucchini al Forno

Use zucchini (courgettes) that are 6 inches (15 cm) long.
This preparation is also very good for thin Italian or Japanese
eggplants (aubergines). Peel, salt, and drain the eggplants for
30 minutes before baking.

Serves 4

1 onion, minced

¼ teaspoon crushed red pepper flakes, or to taste

4 cloves garlic, slivered

2 tablespoons (30 mL) olive oil

2 pounds (907 g) fresh or canned tomatoes, chopped (see
    page 13)

¼ cup (5 g) loosely packed chopped Italian parsley leaves

Salt to taste

4 zucchini (courgettes)

¼ cup (43 g) coarsely grated Parmesan

Heat the onion, crushed red pepper, and garlic in the olive oil over
medium heat. When the onion is soft, after about 5 minutes, add the
tomatoes, parsley, and salt. Lower heat, cover, and cook 10 minutes.
Preheat the oven to 350°F (180°C/gas 4).
Remove the ends of the zucchini, but do not peel them. Place them
in a lightly oiled baking dish that is small enough so they can be arranged
tightly. Spoon the tomato sauce over them. Bake, uncovered, for 4 minutes, until zucchini are sizzling hot but still firm. Serve hot.

76
Stuffed Eggplant
Melanzane Ripiene

Often flavored with anchovies, these stuffed eggplants
(aubergines) are fully vegetarian with a very tasty stuffing of
roasted peppers (capsicums), garlic, onion, sundried
tomatoes, black olives, pine nuts, and spices. If you are

missing one or two of these ingredients, proceed anyway. When scooping out the eggplants, be careful not to poke holes in the skins.

Serves 4

2 eggplants (aubergines), about 1 pound (454 g) each
Salt
2 red bell peppers (capsicums)
¼ cup (59 mL) olive oil
2 cloves garlic, pressed or minced finely
¼ teaspoon crushed red pepper flakes, or to taste
1 cup (156 g) chopped red (Spanish) onion
4 plum tomatoes, peeled and chopped (see page 13)
6 sundried tomatoes packed in oil, pitted and chopped
6 black olives packed in oil, pitted and chopped
¼ cup (46 g) coarsely chopped pine nuts (chopping can be done in a blender)
¼ cup (5 g) loosely packed minced Italian parsley
12 large basil leaves, julienned
½ teaspoon dried oregano
¾ cup (128 g) grated Parmesan, locatelli, or pecorino cheese
1 cup (128 g) unseasoned dried bread crumbs (see page 28)
Basic Tomato Sauce (page 48) (optional)

Slice eggplants lengthwise and, using a sharp knife, cut out the pulp, leaving ¼-inch (.6 cm) shells. Rub salt into them and let sit on a plate, skin sides up, to drain. Dice the pulp into ½-inch (1 cm) cubes, salt, and let drain in a colander for 30 minutes. Roast the bell peppers (see page 25). Cut them into 1-inch (2.5 cm) squares.

Preheat the oven to 350°F (180°C/gas 4).

Gently squeeze excess water from the cubed eggplant and wipe off any remaining salt. Heat the oil over medium-high heat and sauté the garlic and crushed red pepper for 1 minute, then add the onion. Sauté for about 5 minutes, or until the onion is soft and transparent. Add the eggplant and sauté for 2 or 3 minutes, until it is soft. Remove from the heat. Add the tomatoes, sundried tomatoes, olives, pine nuts, parsley, basil, oregano, ½ cup of the cheese, the roasted peppers, and the bread crumbs and stir. Divide this mixture among the eggplant shells. Top each with a generous amount of grated cheese and place in an oiled baking dish. Bake uncovered for 30 minutes. Serve at room temperature as an antipasto, or hot, with and without tomato sauce, as a main course.

77
Eggplant Parmesan
Melanzane alla Parmigiana

Nothing delicate or *nuovo*, this dish is one of the most filling vegetable main dishes ever. You can serve squares of it over lasagna noodles that have been cooked and tossed with finely chopped tomatoes, basil leaves, and olive oil. It is also great in sandwiches and small slices can be served as appetizers.

It is good served hot, at room temperature, or, in the summer, it can even be served cold. You will need a 7 by 11-inch (18 by 28 cm) baking dish or its equivalent to make this recipe. (You should get three layers.)

Serves 4 as a main dish

2 pounds (907 g) eggplant (aubergines)
Salt
1 clove garlic, pressed or minced
¼ teaspoon crushed red pepper flakes, or to taste
1 tablespoon (15 mL) olive oil, plus additional for frying, enough to come to a generous ¼-inch (.6 cm) deep in frying pan
2 pounds (907 g) canned or fresh tomatoes, peeled and chopped (see page 13)
6 whole fresh basil leaves, or ½ teaspoon dried basil
1 teaspoon dried oregano
1 tablespoon (16 g) tomato paste
1 cup (184 g) unbleached all-purpose (plain) flour
3 eggs, beaten
8 ounces (227 g) mozzarella, thinly sliced
¼ cup (43 g) grated Parmesan

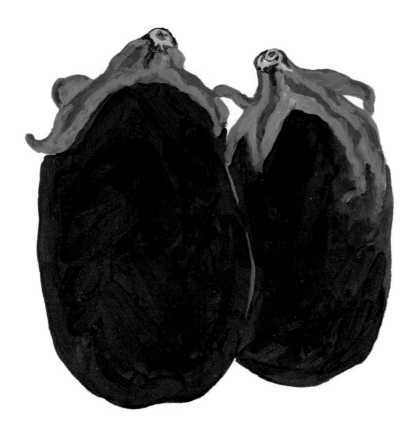

Peel the eggplant and cut them lengthwise in ¼-inch (.6 cm)-thick slices. Place the sliced eggplant in a colander, sprinkle generously with salt, making sure all surfaces are covered, and let drain for 30 minutes.

Meanwhile, make a tomato sauce. Heat the garlic and crushed red pepper in a pot with the 1 tablespoon of olive oil. When they are hot, add the tomatoes, basil, oregano, and tomato paste and simmer gently for 10 minutes. If the sauce is too watery, add more tomato paste.

Gently squeeze any extra water out of the eggplant slices and wipe off any remaining salt. Coat each slice with flour and dip in egg, allowing excess egg to drain back into the bowl. Heat the frying oil over high heat until it is quite hot but not smoking, then slide in the eggplant slices. Fry in batches until golden, about 1 or 2 minutes each side. Drain on paper towels.

Preheat the oven to 400°F (200°C/gas 6).

Place a layer of eggplant slices along the bottom of the baking dish. They may overlap. Top this with one third of the mozzarella slices, a sprinkling of Parmesan, and one third of the tomato sauce. Build three layers in this order; the top layer should be sauce.

Bake until top is brown and crusty, about 30 minutes. Let sit for 15 minutes before serving.

78
Mixed Fried Vegetables
Verdura Fritto Misto

If your children will not even look at vegetables, here is a
way to introduce them. Breading and frying seals in the
flavor of vegetables and makes them soft on the inside and
crunchy on the outside. This recipe serves four as a main
course, but fried vegetables make a good appetizer too.
The vegetables can be prepared and breaded ahead of time,
but should be served immediately after frying. Precooking
the vegetables insures a quick, even fry. (It is not necessary
to precook the mushrooms.) Broccoli can be substituted for
cauliflower, but boil it a bit less. Canned or frozen artichoke
hearts can be substituted for fresh (no need to boil these, but
thaw thoroughly if they are frozen). Please feel free to make
whatever substitutions or additions you wish. Vegetables
should be prepared and allowed to cool before breading.

Makes 36 pieces: serves 4 as a main course

1 zucchini (courgette)

6 spears asparagus

6 cauliflower florets, approximately 1 inch (2.5 cm) in
diameter

1 large artichoke

Lemon juice

6 mushrooms, 1 inch (2.5 cm) each, washed, dried, and
stems trimmed

½ cup (92 g) unbleached all-purpose (plain) flour

2 cups (255 g) dried bread crumbs (see page 28)

3 eggs

¼ cup (59 mL) beer

1 teaspoon dried oregano

¼ cup (5 g) loosely packed finely chopped Italian parsley

2 tablespoons (43 g) grated Parmesan, pecorino, or loeatelli
cheese

Salt to taste

½ teaspoon crushed red pepper flakes, or to taste

Vegetable oil for frying (olive oil mixed in equal parts with
corn, safflower, or soybean oil) to come to a generous ½
inch (1 cm) deep in the pan

Lemon wedges, for garnish

Cut zucchini into 12 wedges: in half lengthwise, then widthwise, then each quarter cut in three. Steam over boiling water for 2 minutes. Break the tough bottoms from the asparagus. Steam the remaining spears whole over boiling water for 2 minutes. Boil cauliflower florets for 2 minutes.

Take out the heart of the artichokes as described on page 23. Discard the leaves. Cut the heart into 6 wedges and boil for 1 minute in water to which lemon juice has been added. Soak in ice water with lemon until ready to use.

When vegetables are cool, bread them and the mushrooms. At a work station with a suitable amount of space, put the flour and the bread crumbs on separate large flat plates. Break the eggs into a large bowl. Add the beer, oregano, parsley, cheese, salt, and crushed red pepper to the eggs and beat well.

Roll each vegetable piece in the flour, then the egg mixture, and finally the bread crumbs, seeing that it is completely covered at each turn. Have all the vegetables prepared before beginning to fry them.

Heat the oil for frying in a pan over high heat. When it is very hot but not smoking, begin putting in the vegetable pieces in batches. Do not crowd too many pieces into the pan—it will lower the oil temperature. When the vegetables' undersides are golden brown (about 1 minute), turn them over and fry until the other side is golden brown. Remove from oil with a slotted spoon and drain on paper towels or brown paper. Keep fried vegetables warm while you are frying the rest.

79
Batter-Fried Vegetables
Verdura Fritto all'Aceto

Certain vegetables, like fennel, broccoli rabe, and zucchini
(courgettes) lend themselves well to batter-frying. Eaten
with a sharp vinegar dressing, this dish is quite a bit like
Japanese tempura. Unless you grow them yourselves,
zucchini flowers are not that easy to find. Slices of raw
zucchini or bell pepper (capsicum) can be substituted if you
cannot find the flowers. One caveat: since batter-fried
vegetables must be served hot and crisp and because they
get soggy faster than those that are breaded and fried, they
are difficult to make in large quantities as a main course—
impossible if the cook expects to sit down and eat with the
guests.

Serves 4 as an appetizer, 2 as a main course

1 fennel bulb

8 spears broccoli rabe

1½ cups (355 mL) beer (1 bottle)

½ teaspoon salt

1½ cups (376 g) unbleached all-purpose (plain) flour

8 zucchini (courgette) flowers, washed

**Vegetable oil for frying (olive oil mixed in equal parts with
corn, safflower, or soybean oil) to come to 1 inch (2.5)
deep in the pan**

Balsamic vinegar or good quality wine vinegar, for dipping

Cut away the fennel tops and tough outer skin. Leave the base on the
bulb. Cut the inner bulb vertically into ½-inch (1 cm)-thick slices. Trim
the bottoms of the slices, leaving enough of the base intact that the slices
will still hold together. Trim the tough lower stems from the broccoli
rabe spears.

In a bowl, mix the beer with salt and flour. (Lumps don't matter.) Keep
this batter and the prepared vegetables ready at hand near the stove.

Heat the oil for frying in a suitably deep pot over high heat. When the
oil is hot but not smoking, dip the fennel slices in the batter and place
them in the hot oil so that pieces are touching but not overlapping. Fry
until golden and crisp, about 2 minutes. Proceed similarly with broccoli
rabe and zucchini blossoms or other vegetables. Serve hot, with the vinegar for dipping.

80
Baked Stuffed Mushrooms
Funghi Cini al Forno

Use portabello mushroom caps for this. Try to find caps that
are at least 4 inches (10 cm) in diameter. If using ordinary
mushrooms, choose the largest ones. Whatever the size,
altogether you should have about 1 pound. Select
mushrooms with stems and caps intact.

Serves 4

1 pound (454 g) portabello mushrooms
5 tablespoons (74 mL) olive oil
½ cup (64 g) unseasoned dried bread crumbs (see page 28)
¼ cup (43 g) grated pecorino, locatelli, or Parmesan cheese
¼ cup (5 g) finely chopped Italian parsley
½ teaspoon dried rosemary
1 clove garlic, pressed or finely minced
2 tablespoons (30 mL) balsamic vinegar
Salt to taste
¼ teaspoon crushed red pepper flakes, or to taste

Rinse the mushrooms under cold water and pat them dry. Remove the
stems and set aside the caps. Discard the fibrous bottoms of the stems,
and chop what remains of the stems small. Briefly sauté the chopped
stems in 1 tablespoon (15 mL) olive oil over medium heat until they are
reduced, about 2 or 3 minutes.

Preheat the oven to 400°F (200°C/gas 6).

In a bowl, mix the sautéed stems, bread crumbs, cheese, parsley, rosemary, 3 tablespoons (44 mL) olive oil, garlic, vinegar, salt, and crushed
red pepper.

Place the mushroom caps skin side down in an oiled baking dish. Stuff
them by spooning the bread crumbs into the mushrooms. Dribble remaining olive oil on top. Bake for about 30 minutes, until the mushrooms
are sizzling and the top of the stuffing is brown. Serve hot.

81
Grilled Vegetables
Verdura Griglia Mista

You may grill vegetables under the kitchen broiler (grill), but their flavor improves by a quantum leap when they are sizzled over a wood or charcoal fire. Serve grilled vegetables by themselves, with good bread, or over cooked lasagna noodles that have been dressed with finely chopped tomatoes and olive oil. Leftover grilled vegetables are excellent with cheese in sandwiches or cut up and tossed with pasta such as rigatoni.

If you are preparing a mixed grill that also includes meat or fish, vegetables can go on the coals first because they do not need to be eaten hot. Use more coals than you would for meat alone. Because of the bulk of the vegetables, and their negligible fat quantity, the fire doesn't spit at them; small amounts of marinade should be spooned over them so they sizzle.

Serves 4 heavy eaters as a main dish

1 large eggplant (aubergine)

Salt

2 onions

1 bulb fennel

2 ripe tomatoes

2 zucchini (courgettes)

4 portabello mushroom caps

2 red bell peppers (capsicums)

Marinade

½ cup (118 mL) olive oil

½ cup (118 mL) wine vinegar

1 teaspoon crushed red pepper flakes

3 cloves garlic, pressed or finely minced

1 tablespoon oregano

1 teaspoon (7 g) salt

Optional Pasta and Sauce

2 tablespoons (15 mL) olive oil

1 pound (454 g) fresh or canned tomatoes, peeled and chopped small

6 fresh basil leaves

1 pound (454 g) lasagna noodles, broken in half, or 1 pound (454 g) rigatoni

Cut the unpeeled eggplant lengthwise into ½-inch (1 cm)-thick slices. Salt generously and allow to drain in a colander for 30 minutes.

Cut the onions in half lengthwise. Remove the outer skin but not the root stem, so the halves hold together. Trim the fennel bulbs of their leafy tops and hard outer layers, leaving the base intact. Cut lengthwise in ½-inch (1 cm) slices. Cut the tomatoes in half lengthwise.

Cut the zucchini lengthwise into ½-inch (1 cm) slices. Do not peel. Wash and dry the mushroom caps.

In a large baking dish, whisk together the oil, vinegar, crushed red pepper, garlic, oregano, and salt. Put all vegetables except the bell peppers in the marinade for an hour or two, gently basting or rotating every 15 minutes.

While the vegetables are marinating, cut the bell peppers in half, removing the stems and seeds. Do not marinate them.

Prepare the fire. When coals are hot (or oven broiler [grill] is well preheated), place the onion and pepper halves on first, skin side down. They will take a little longer to cook. Three to five minutes later, put the eggplant and zucchini slices, tomatoes, and mushrooms on the grill. Sear all vegetables except the peppers on one side and turn them. The peppers are done when their skin is blackened. Peel the skin and dress the peppers with a drizzle of olive oil.

To make the optional pasta, heat the 2 tablespoons of oil over medium heat in a saucepan. Add the tomatoes and basil, stir, remove from heat, and let sit. Cook the pasta until al dente, drain, return to the pan and warm through with the tomato sauce.

Arrange all the vegetables on a huge platter. If serving with pasta, serve individual portions of pasta and let eaters help themselves to different combinations.

Variation: Vegetables cooked directly in hot embers are also delicious: they become caramelized. Fennel is especially good this way. Clean the fennel of tops, bottom, and outer layers. Slice the bulb in quarters lengthwise. Anoint each quarter lightly with olive oil, then wrap tightly in heavy-duty aluminum foil. Place in the hottest part of the embers and cook for 30 to 40 minutes. You can cook cauliflower, zucchini, or broccoli similarly.

131

82
Stuffed Peppers
Pipicini

While red bell peppers (capsicums) are preferred for
roasting, green are usually used for stuffing because the flesh
gets a bit softer in the oven. However, if you prefer, you can
use red, yellow, or orange peppers in the recipe below.
Whatever their color, use symmetrical peppers.
There are two ways to stuff peppers: either cut off the tops
and remove the seeds and ribs, fill the entire cavity with the
stuffing, and bake upright; or cut the peppers in half
lengthwise and place the horizontal halves in the baking pan.
I prefer the latter: the peppers cook more thoroughly and
they are easier to eat and serve.
If you are using canned tomatoes for the sauce, use ¾ cup
(177 mL) of the juice you drain off to cook the rice.

Serves 4

1½ cups (355 mL) Vegetable Broth (page 36)

or

¾ cup (177 mL) tomato juice mixed with ¾ cup (177 mL)
  water

1 tablespoon (15 mL) olive oil

¾ cup (170 g) Arborio rice

½ tablespoon (1 g) butter

Salt to taste

Sauce

2 cloves garlic, crushed or minced

½ teaspoon crushed red pepper flakes, or to taste

4 tablespoons (59 mL) olive oil

2 pounds (907 g) fresh or canned tomatoes, peeled and
  chopped (see page 13)

6 whole fresh basil leaves or ¼ teaspoon dried

1 cup (128 g) unseasoned dried bread crumbs (see page 28)

2 eggs, hard-boiled, peeled, and chopped

1 egg, beaten

2 tablespoons capers

4 ounces (113 g) provolone, grated

½ teaspoon oregano

4 large bell peppers (capsicums), about 2 pounds (907 g)

Bring the vegetable broth or tomato juice and water to a boil. In a separate pot, heat 1 tablespoon (15 mL) of the olive oil over medium heat. Add the rice and stir, coating the grains in the oil. Pour in the boiling stock or juice and add the butter and salt. Cover and cook over low heat for 15 minutes. Remove from heat. Leave covered. Allow to cool while you make the sauce.

To make the sauce, heat the garlic and ¼ teaspoon crushed red pepper in 2 tablespoons (30 mL) of the olive oil in a pot over high heat. Add the tomatoes and stir briefly. Then add basil, cover, and cook for 15 minutes on low heat.

Meanwhile, toast the bread crumbs in a pan over medium-high heat until they are golden, about 2 minutes. Place them in a large bowl and mix in the hard-boiled eggs, beaten egg, capers, provolone, oregano, ¼ teaspoon crushed red pepper, and 1 tablespoon (15 mL) of olive oil. Then add the rice and mix again.

Preheat the oven to 350°F (180°C)/gas 4).

Wash the peppers and *either* cut the tops off as near to the stem as possible *or* cut them in half lengthwise. In either case, discard the stem base and remove seeds and ribs. Rub them inside and out with the remaining tablespoon of olive oil. Arrange in a baking dish, spoon in the rice mixture, and cover the tops with a thin layer of the tomato sauce. Bake for 45 minutes, until pepper skins begin to soften and sag. Reheat remaining tomato sauce and serve with the peppers.

83
Grilled Stuffed Mushrooms
Funghi alla Griglia

In this recipe for stuffed mushrooms, the caps are grilled rather than baked. Select mushrooms with large caps, slightly concave at the gills. Use a blender or food processor to chop the pine nuts.

Serves 4

1 pound (454 g) portabello mushrooms
¼ cup (59 mL) wine vinegar or balsamic vinegar
½ teaspoon dried rosemary
6 tablespoons (89 mL) olive oil
2 cloves garlic, pressed or minced
¼ teaspoon crushed red pepper flakes, or to taste
4 cups (340 g) trimmed, washed, dried, and chopped
    arugula (rocket) (about two medium bunches)
Salt to taste
¼ cup (46 g) coarsely chopped pine nuts
3 tablespoons (44 mL) freshly squeezed lemon juice
2 tablespoons (21 g) grated Parmesan, pecorino, or locatelli
    cheese

Rinse the mushrooms under cold water and pat them dry. If the mushrooms have stems, remove them entirely, cut away their tough bottoms, and mince what is left, reserving the caps. Mix the vinegar and rosemary with 4 tablespoons (59 ml) of the olive oil and marinate.

Place the remaining olive oil in a pan with the garlic and crushed pepper over high heat. When the garlic sizzles, add the arugula and minced mushroom stems (if any), and quickly stir-fry for about 2 or 3 minutes, until the greens are thoroughly wilted. Add the salt, pine nuts, and lemon juice, stir, remove from heat, and set aside.

Preheat the broiler (grill). Place the mushroom in a baking dish top side up and broil for 6 minutes. Turn them over so their top sides are down and broil for 4 minutes. Remove from the broiler and fill the caps with the arugula and pine nut mixture. Sprinkle cheese over each and return to broil for 3 or 4 minutes, until the topping is brown and the mushrooms are bubbling hot. Serve hot as a main course with bread and salad, or, if they are a starter or appetizer, serve mushrooms hot or at room temperature.

84
Mixed Vegetable Stew
La Fritella

This is a spring vegetable stew that goes well with rice or pasta but is usually served with bread. If you wish to reduce preparation time drastically, use one 10-ounce package of frozen artichokes, thawed, or a 14-ounce (400 g) can of artichoke hearts, drained. If fava (broad) beans are not available, use lima beans. If fresh peas are not available, use frozen.

Serves 4

4 large artichokes

2 lemons

1 fennel bulb

1 pound (454 g) asparagus

¼ cup (59 mL) olive oil

3 plum tomatoes, peeled and chopped (see page 13)

1 pound (454 g) fresh fava (broad) beans, shelled and peeled to yield about 1 cup (184 g) beans

1 pound (454 g) fresh peas, shelled to yield about 1 cup (184 g) peas, or 5 ounces (142 g) frozen peas, thawed

Salt to taste

4 ounces (113 g) provolone, sliced or shaved

Clean the artichokes down to their hearts (see page 31). Cut each heart into 6 wedges. In a bowl, cover these in water that contains the juice of 1 lemon (save a little of the juice for later). Remove the top, bottom, and the outer layers from the fennel. Chop the bulb into large pieces. Cut the tough lower ends from the asparagus stalks and chop the stalks into 1½-inch (4 cm) lengths.

Heat the olive oil in a large pot over medium heat. Add the artichokes, the fennel, and the tomatoes and stir to coat them all with the oil. Lower the heat and add a small squirt of lemon juice. Cover and cook over low heat for 10 minutes. (If you are using canned or frozen artichokes, less cooking time is needed.) Check from time to time; if the vegetables are dry, add a tablespoon of water or tomato juice. Take care that the stew does not become soupy.

Add the asparagus and stir in thoroughly. Cover and cook for another 7 minutes, until the asparagus begins to soften. Add the fava beans and the peas. Cover and cook for another 5 minutes, until all the vegetables are tender but still crisp.

Serve with lemon wedges and sliced provolone on the table. If serving with pasta or rice, shave the cheese.

85
Orzo-Stuffed Tomatoes
Pomodori Ripiene

Orzo is barley-shaped pasta—essentially it is no different from *riso*. In this recipe it is precooked briefly and then brought to a perfectly al dente state in the tomato shell. As it cooks, it expands, so don't pack the tomatoes too tightly with the stuffing or they will burst. If you have extra stuffing, place it in a covered pan and bake it. Use only red, ripe, fresh tomatoes.

Serves 4

4 good-sized tomatoes, about 2 pounds (907 g) total weight
¼ cup (28 g) orzo
Salt
1 clove garlic, pressed or finely minced
¼ cup (37 g) minced onion
8 basil leaves, chopped
¼ cup (5 g) loosely packed finely chopped Italian parsley leaves
1 teaspoon oregano
¼ cup (48 g) grated Parmesan, pecorino, or locatelli cheese
2 tablespoons (30 mL) olive oil
¼ teaspoon crushed red pepper flakes, or to taste

Wash the tomatoes and cut off the top ¼ inch (.6 cm) of each. Set the tops aside. Scoop out the seeds and inner flesh. (A grapefruit spoon works well for this.) Depending on the tomato, you should have about ¼ inch (.6 cm) to ½ inch (1 cm) of pulp next to the skin. Set what you scoop out in a colander for 10 minutes, allowing the juice to drain. Discard what seeds you can, using the colander as a sieve. Then chop the remaining tomato flesh into small pieces.

Preheat the oven to 400°F (200°C/gas 6).

Boil the orzo in salted water for 4 minutes. Drain. In a bowl, combine the orzo with the chopped tomato flesh. Then add all the remaining ingredients and salt to taste and mix thoroughly. Fill the tomato shells with the mixture. Remember not to pack the shells, as the orzo will expand as it cooks. Put the tops back on the tomato shells and arrange them in an oiled baking pan. Cover and bake for 20 to 25 minutes. Serve hot.

86
Potato Casserole
Timballo di Patati

Another way to serve vegetables is in a *timballo* or casserole. Originally this was a custard-like dish made with cheese and eggs and baked in a drum-shaped pastry mold. In Sicily this is called a *sformata* (mold) and is usually baked with a crust of eggs and bread crumbs on the bottom so it can be tapped out upside down onto a plate. But there are many simple variations, as is this recipe, where potatoes, seasonings, and cheese are simply put in a baking dish, topped with bread crumbs, baked, and served top-side up. If you wish, you may use the crust used for Cauliflower Casserole (page 138) to make this easy-to-prepare and filling favorite a bit different.

Serves 4
¼ cup (59 mL) olive oil
2 pounds (907 g) potatoes, sliced in ¼-inch (.6 cm) rounds
1 onion, thinly sliced
Salt to taste
¼ teaspoon crushed red pepper flakes, or to taste
8 ounces (227 g) ricotta
4 ounces (113 g) mozzarella, grated
2 tablespoons (23 g) unbleached all-purpose (plain) flour
1 cup (287 mL) cool water
¼ teaspoon nutmeg
1 teaspoon rosemary
1 cup (128 g) unseasoned dried bread crumbs (see page 28)

Oil the bottom of a baking dish with 1 tablespoon (15 mL) of the olive oil. Place half the potatoes into the dish, then half the onions. Season with salt and crushed red pepper. Spread on half the ricotta, sprinkle with half the mozzarella and drizzle on a tablespoon of olive oil. Repeat the process for a second layer, up to but not including the olive oil.

Preheat the oven to 350°F (180°C/gas 4).

Put the remaining 2 tablespoons (30 mL) of olive oil in a small saucepan. Add the flour and mix gently, heating over medium heat for 1 minute or so. Do not let the flour burn or get brown in any way. Add the water, nutmeg, and rosemary, and bring to a boil over medium heat, stirring constantly. Smooth lumps with a whisk or press them out with a wooden spoon. Pour this white sauce over the potatoes and onions. Top with the bread crumbs and bake uncovered for 1 hour, until the top is brown and crusty and the rest is thoroughly melted and bubbling hot. Let sit for 5 to 10 minutes before serving.

87
Cauliflower Casserole
Sformata di Cavalfiore

Sformata is a dish that has many variations and is usually made with several eggs and plenty of cheeses in a ring mold. After baking, the *sformata* is tapped out, and the center can be filled with such delicacies as marinated artichoke hearts, lightly cooked peas, sliced hard-boiled eggs, blanched fava (broad) beans, or roasted red bell peppers (capsicums). Here is an example using cauliflower and ricotta cheese. Broccoli will work well in place of the cauliflower. If you use broccoli, you will need to reduce the initial boiling time by half, as it cooks more quickly.

If you don't have a 10 inch (25 cm) ring mold, a large loaf
pan will serve for baking. As you can make the recipe
for Potato Casserole more complicated, you can simplify this
one: oil the pan, pour in the vegetables, cheese, and
seasonings, put the bread crumbs (without the egg) on top,
and bake.

Serves 4

1 head cauliflower, cut into florets
1 potato, cut in quarters
1 onion, minced
¼ teaspoon crushed red pepper flakes, or to taste
2 tablespoons (28 g) butter
2 tablespoons (23 g) unbleached all-purpose (plain) flour
¼ teaspoon nutmeg
8 ounces (227 g) ricotta
¼ cup (43 g) grated Parmesan, locatelli, or pecorino cheese
½ cup (64 g) unseasoned dried bread crumbs (see page 28)
2 eggs

Place the cauliflower and potato in enough water to cover and boil for
10 minutes or so, until they are soft. Drain and set aside, saving a cup
(237 mL) of water for the sauce in this recipe. (You may reserve the rest
for stock, if you like.)

Sauté the onion and crushed red pepper in the olive oil until the onion
is soft, about 5 minutes. Add the cauliflower and the potato and sauté,
mashing the cauliflower and potato as you do. When the mixture is pasty,
remove it from the pot and set it aside.

Preheat the oven to 350°F (180°C/gas 4).

Using the same pot (no need to clean it), melt the butter. Add the flour
and stir to form a paste. Add the reserved cup of the cauliflower cooking
water and the nutmeg. Over medium heat, bring the mixture to a slow
boil, stirring and mashing out lumps all the while. This will take 3 or
4 minutes. Remove from the heat and put the potato-cauliflower-onion
mixture back in the pot with the sauce. Mix in the cheeses.

Oil a ring or ovenproof casserole. Add half the bread crumbs, shaking
the pan back and forth and tilting it to distribute the crumbs evenly. Pour
out any loose crumbs. Beat 1 egg and pour it into the pan. Again, tilt the
pan back and forth to distribute all along the bottom and sides. Add a second layer of bread crumbs on top of the egg. Beat the second egg and add
it to the cooled potato-cauliflower-cheese mixture. Pour it all into the bread
crumb–crusted baking pan.

Bake for 45 minutes. After removing from oven, allow casserole to
set for at least 15 minutes before turning over and tapping out onto a
serving platter.

88
Sicilian Falafel
Crespelli di Ceci

Arabs, Greeks, and Turks all have their tiles in the mosaic of
Sicilian cooking. In the northwest, around Trapani and Erice,
ceci panini (chickpea sandwiches) or *fave panini* (fava [broad]
bean sandwiches) are offered on many menus. Very similar to
the Middle Eastern standby falafel, the Sicilian specialty is
normally served on buns of country wheat bread, often
topped with Sautéed Greens (see page 21) or slices of raw
tomato, and dressed with a squirt of lemon juice and a slather
of Mayonnaise (see page 116), or fresh ricotta.

These *crespelli* should have a crunchy texture all the way
through. The chickpeas are not cooked, but merely soaked
so they approximate raw, fresh chickpeas. If you use fresh fava
beans, remove them from their pods, dip in boiling water,
and remove the inner skins. You'll need about 2 cups (396 g).

If you use canned chickpeas, the result will be a little
mushier—quite edible, as bean-burgers go, but lacking
Mediterranean gusto. A 19-ounce (539 g) can will yield
approximately 2 cups, the same volume as 1 cup (148 g)
dried chickpeas, soaked. Only add the egg if you feel your mix
will not hold up to frying. (Have faith, it probably will.)

Makes 8 crespelli: serves 4

1 cup (148 g) dried chickpeas, or 2 cups (396 g) canned

2 tablespoons (31 g) pine nuts

½ cup (10 g) loosely packed chopped Italian parsley

2 cloves garlic, minced or crushed

½ cup (28 g) chopped onion

1 teaspoon cumin

1 teaspoon dried coriander seeds

¼ teaspoon crushed red pepper flakes, or to taste

Salt to taste

½ cup (92 g) semolina or unbleached all-purpose (plain)
flour

1 teaspoon (7 g) baking powder

1 egg (optional)

Oil for frying (olive oil mixed with vegetable oil to come to ¼
inch [.6 cm] deep in the pan)

Lemon wedges, mayonnaise, or fresh ricotta to serve

Either soak the chickpeas in cold water overnight or try this quicker method: bring 4 cups (946 mL) of unsalted water to a boil in a heavy pot. Add the chickpeas. Boil for 5 minutes, remove from heat, and let sit covered for 2 hours. They will be perfectly al dente, as they should be for this recipe.

Drain the chickpeas. (Save the water for soup stock if you like.) Place the chickpeas in a blender or food processor and chop them up coarsely. They should not be smoothly puréed, but in small pieces the size of cracked wheat. Do the same with the pine nuts and combine them with the chickpeas in a large bowl. Put the parsley, garlic, onion, cumin, coriander, crushed red pepper, and salt in the blender and process as smooth as you can. Add this mixture to the bowl.

Add the flour and baking powder and mix well. If you are using an egg, beat it and add it at this time. The mixture should be stiff and cohesive. Form 8 firm patties about ¾ inch (2 cm) thick and 3 inches (8 cm) in diameter. Heat oil for frying in a 10-inch/25 cm pan over high heat. Fry patties for about 5 minutes, until they are golden brown on both sides. Remove from pan and drain on brown paper or paper towels. Serve *crespellis* in sandwiches or as is, with lemon, mayonnaise, or fresh ricotta.

89
Fried Mozzarella Sandwiches
Mozzarella in Carrozza

"Mozzarella in a Carriage" is a traditional starter, but now seems a rather heavy appetizer for today's tastes. Delicious nonetheless, it makes a filling lunch. Use fresh mozzarella, if you can. This is the perfect use for slices of stale bread.
Other things can be added to these sandwiches, such as Sautéed Spinach (page 21), sundried tomatoes, or strips of roasted peppers (capsicums), page 25. Use a small (6-inch/15 cm) skillet so the oil will have some depth.

Serves 4

8 (¼-inch/.6 cm) slices fresh or stale crusty bread

4 (¼-inch/.6 cm) slices mozzarella, the approximate dimensions of the bread slices

½ cup (118 mL) olive oil

½ cup (92 g) unbleached all-purpose (plain) flour

1 egg, beaten (you may need 2 if the bread slices are large)

Make sandwiches of the bread and mozzarella, laying one slice of mozzarella between two slices of bread.

Heat the oil until it is quite hot. Dust each sandwich with flour and dip in the egg, coating well. Let excess egg drip back into the bowl. Gently slip sandwiches into the hot oil, one by one. Like grilled cheese sandwiches, they may be a little unstable before going into the pan, but as the egg cooks and the cheese melts they will hold together nicely. Fry until both sides are golden brown, about 1 minute per side.

Remove from pan and drain on paper towels. Serve immediately.

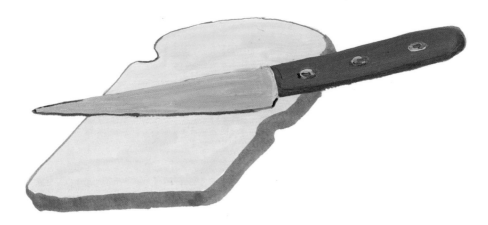

IX
Salads
Insalate

In Sicily, salad is often served following the main course. It is made from any green leaf lettuce, such as romaine (cos). Escarole, arugula (rocket), radicchio, and endive (chicory) are also used. The greens are washed, dried, and their coarse stems are removed; then they are chilled, chopped or ripped by hand, and seasoned with salt and freshly ground black pepper. Finally, they are tossed with oil and wine vinegar in the proportion of two parts oil to one part vinegar.

The following recipes are for more substantial salads, and lean a bit towards American tastes. Many recipes in the appetizers section of this book can be used in green salads to give them some zest; try adding small bits of marinated vegetables, roasted peppers (capsicums), or beets, marinated mozzarella, or fava (broad) beans. Likewise, the following salads can be served in a variety of ways: before or after the main course; or as main courses themselves.

Whatever place it has in the meal, salad is good only when it is fresh. Always use the best quality olive oil and the finest vinegar you can find.

90
Fennel, Orange, and Mozzarella Salad
Insalata di Finocchio, Aranci, e Formaggio

Here, citrus is substituted for vinegar in the salad dressing. This makes a fine starter or a post–main course salad. Use navel or other large eating oranges, or if you can find blood oranges, use them by all means. Fresh mozzarella is best.

Serves 4

1 fennel bulb
1 large orange, or 2 small
2 ounces (57 g) mozzarella
2 tablespoons finely chopped Italian parsley
¼ teaspoon crushed red pepper flakes, or to taste
Salt to taste
¼ cup (59 mL) olive oil

Trim the base and remove the coarse outer layers of the fennel. Discard the tops, saving ¼ cup of the finest green leaves, chopped fine. Slice the bulb horizontally into the thinnest slices possible. Peel the orange and slice it horizontally into the thinnest slices possible. Poke out seeds, if any. Slice the mozzarella as thin as possible. Cut the slices into ¼ inch (.6 cm) strips. Add the parsley, crushed red pepper, and salt. Toss all the ingredients with the olive oil. Use the chopped fennel leaves as garnish, and serve.

91
Potato–String Bean Salad
Insalata di Patati e Fagiolini

Boiling times can vary for string beans depending on their size and freshness, from 3 minutes for the thin beans (haricots verts) to 10 minutes for regular string beans. The beans should be firm, but cooked. This salad can be eaten as is or served on a bed of washed and dried arugula (rocket) leaves, garnished with thin slices of hard-boiled egg.

Serves 4

1 pound string beans, washed, ends trimmed, and cut into pieces 1½ inches (4 cm) long

Salt to taste

¼ cup (59 mL) olive oil

¼ cup (59 mL) red wine or balsamic vinegar

¼ cup (39 g) finely chopped red (Spanish) onion

1 tablespoon capers

1 tablespoon finely chopped Italian parsley

¼ teaspoon crushed red pepper flakes, or to taste

1 pound (454 g) potatoes

1 bunch arugula (rocket)

1 hard-boiled egg, for garnish

Place the string beans in 8 cups (1.9 L) of boiling salted water until cooked. Remove beans from the boiling water with a slotted spoon. Let them sit a minute in a colander. Save the water.

While the beans are cooking, mix the olive oil, vinegar, onion, capers, parsley, salt to taste, and crushed red pepper together in a large bowl. Place drained beans in the dressing and mix well while they are still warm.

Peel the potatoes and quarter them lengthwise into wedges, then cut the wedges into ¼-inch (.6 cm) slices. Bring the water that the beans were cooked in back to a boil and add the potatoes. Potatoes should cook 3 to 5 minutes, depending on thickness, length, and width, until they are cooked but firm enough so they will not fall apart. Check them often. Drain and add them to the bowl with the string beans and the dressing. Toss gently but thoroughly and let sit unrefrigerated for 30 minutes before serving.

92
Provolone Salad
Insalata Rusticana

In Sicily this simple farm salad is made with *caciocavallo* cheese. Since *caciocavallo* is not widely available, substitute provolone. Use imported chunk provolone, not slices; or substitute feta cheese to make a Greek salad. The vegetables should be cut in robust chucks, anointed with oil but no vinegar, and tossed with plenty of dried oregano. The cucumber must be crisp, the tomato ripe and firm.

Serves 4

1 red bell pepper (capsicum), roasted (see page 25)
1 cucumber
1 large tomato
6 ounces (170 g) provolone
¼ cup (39 g) diced red (Spanish) onion
1 tablespoon dried oregano
6 black olives packed in oil, pitted and minced
¼ cup (5 g) loosely packed Italian parsley leaves
¼ cup (59 mL) olive oil

Cut the roasted pepper in thin slices. Peel the cucumber and cut it in four wedges lengthwise. Cut each wedge into 1-inch (2.5 cm) pieces. Cut the tomato into wedges with ½-inch (1 cm) edges. Cut provolone into ½ inch (1 cm) cubes.

Gently toss red pepper, cucumber, tomato, and cheese with onion, oregano, olives, parsley, and olive oil. Serve.

93
Cauliflower-Fennel Salad
Insalata di Cavolfiore e Finocchio

This salad can be made and dressed an hour or two before serving.

Serves 4

1 medium cauliflower
1 fennel bulb, with tops
1 tablespoon capers
10 black olives packed in oil, pitted and halved
3 tablespoons (44 mL) lemon juice
¼ cup (59 mL) olive oil
1 clove garlic, crushed or minced
Salt to taste
¼ teaspoon crushed red pepper flakes, or to taste
½ teaspoon dried oregano
¼ cup (5 g) loosely packed chopped Italian parsley

Wash the cauliflower and cut into 1-inch (2.5 cm) florets. Place in boiling water for 3 minutes, then drain in a colander.

Trim the fennel. Chop the bulb finely; it should yield about 1 cup (20 g). Chop 2 tablespoons of the fennel leaves and save for garnish.

Place the chopped fennel bulb, the capers, the olives, and the cauliflower in a suitable bowl. In a separate bowl, whisk or blend the lemon juice, garlic, salt, crushed red pepper, oregano, and oil together. Pour the dressing over the salad and toss. Garnish with the chopped parsley and reserved fennel leaves, and serve at room temperature.

94

Sicilian Coleslaw with Orange-Rosemary Dressing

Cavolella in Salsa Arance e Rosmarino

Use savoy cabbage if you can. Its crinkled leaves serve to pocket the dressing. This dressing will be enough for about 6 cups (735 g) of shredded cabbage. Nuts can add extra crunch.

Serves 4

1 savoy cabbage

2 carrots

1 clove garlic

½ teaspoon dried oregano

1 teaspoon dried rosemary (1 tablespoon fresh rosemary leaves)

1 tablespoon grated orange zest

4 scallions (spring onions), chopped

¼ teaspoon crushed red pepper flakes

⅓ cup (78 mL) olive oil

¼ cup (59 mL) balsamic vinegar

¼ cup (46 g) chopped pistachio nuts (optional)

Remove the outer leaves and stem base from the cabbage. Slice the leaves extremely thin with a sharp knife or shred them in a food processor. Peel and grate the carrots, and mix them in a bowl with the cabbage.

Place the garlic, oregano, rosemary, orange zest, scallions, crushed red pepper, oil, and vinegar in a blender and blend until smooth. Pour the dressing on the salad, mix well, and garnish with pistachios if you wish.

95
White Bean Salad
Insalata di Cannellini

This recipe calls for dried beans so they can be stewed with
herbs. Try finding the small white navy beans that are
sometimes called pea beans. To make an excellent and
unusual spread for bread and crackers, proceed exactly as
below except cook the beans a little longer. After cooling and
dressing, mash the beans with a fork.

Serves 4

1 cup (198 g) dried white beans
4 cloves garlic, peeled and chopped
1 red (Spanish) onion, chopped
2 carrots, peeled and grated
2 tablespoons fresh thyme or 1 teaspoon dried
8 fresh sage leaves or 1 teaspoon dried
½ teaspoon dried oregano
¼ teaspoon crushed red pepper flakes, or to taste
1 tablespoon grated lemon zest
2 bay leaves
Salt to taste
¼ cup (5 g) loosely packed chopped Italian parsley leaves
¼ cup (59 mL) olive oil
2 tablespoons (30 mL) wine vinegar

Rinse and soak the beans overnight or use this quick soaking method:
wash beans well; place 3 cups (710 mL) of water in a heavy pot and bring
to a boil. Add the beans, cover, and boil for 5 minutes. Remove from the
heat and let sit for 1 hour. The beans will be as soft as if you soaked
them overnight.

Place the beans on the stove in a heavy pot with their soaking water.
Add the garlic, onion, carrots, thyme, sage, oregano, crushed red pepper,
lemon zest, and bay leaves and bring to a slow boil. Cover, lower heat,
and simmer until beans are tender, 45 minutes to 1 hour. Check occasionally. If all the water has been absorbed, add more. Do not overcook.

When beans are just tender, drain off any excess water. (Save it for
stock if you like.) Allow beans to sit a few minutes in a colander or strainer
so they can drain and cool off a bit. Remove bay leaves and, if you used
fresh thyme and sage, any hard stems. Place the beans in a mixing bowl.
Add salt, parsley, oil, and vinegar and toss well. Serve at room temperature.

96
Pasta Salad
Insalata di Pasta

Use different colored pasta for this dish. A combination of green (spinach) and red (tomato) pastas are striking. Fusilli is the recommended shape, although any short pasta will do. Novelty pastas also work well here.

Serves 4

⅓ cup (78 mL) olive oil

3 tablespoons (44 mL) lemon juice

1 tablespoon Dijon mustard

1 whole clove garlic, peeled

¼ cup (5 g) loosely packed Italian parsley leaves

6 fresh basil leaves

Salt to taste

¼ teaspoon crushed red pepper flakes, or to taste

1 cup (198 g) 1-inch (2.5 cm) pieces string beans

½ pound fresh asparagus, cut into 1 inch (2.5 cm) lengths

2 cups (396 g) 1-inch (2.5 cm) broccoli florets

1 zucchini (courgettes) washed, unpeeled, and cut into 1-inch (2.5 cm) julienne

1 cup (184 g) fresh or frozen and thawed baby peas

8 ounces (227 g) pasta

Place the olive oil, lemon juice, mustard, garlic, parsley, basil, salt, and crushed red pepper in a blender or food processor, blending at high speed for 30 seconds.

Bring salted water to a boil in a large pot and add the string beans. Boil 2 to 3 minutes. Add the asparagus and broccoli and boil for 3 minutes. Add the zucchini and peas, then instantly remove from the heat. Remove the vegetables with a slotted spoon or strainer, saving the water to boil the pasta. Place the vegetables in a colander and run briefly under cold water to stop the cooking. They should be tender-crisp. Let sit to drain well, then toss with the dressing.

Bring the water to a boil once again and add the pasta. Cook until al dente. Drain well and toss with the vegetables and dressing, mixing thoroughly. Let stand at room temperature 30 minutes or so, stirring occasionally, to absorb the flavors.

X
Desserts
Dolci

In Sicily, the most common way to end a mean is to have orange wedges, perhaps with a splash of aromatic liqueur. An illogical rule that still somehow makes perfect sense dictates that big feasts are followed by filling desserts, wonderful pastries such as *sfinci*, cheesecake, cannoli, or *sfogiodelle*. Often, no one has room for dessert. No matter; pastry makes an excellent breakfast.

A full examination of the Sicilian sweet tooth is beyond the scope of this book—and perhaps it's just as well. But here are a handful of the best treats.

97
Pine Nut Cookies
Biscotti di Pignoli

Commercially prepared almond paste is made of ground almonds and sugar. These cookies can be made by substituting almonds ground in a blender or food processor. The result will be less sweet and a bit grittier but just as delicious.

Makes about 1 dozen cookies

½ cup (113 g) granulated sugar

½ cup (62 g) confectioners' (icing) sugar, plus additional for dusting

¼ cup (46 g) unsifted unbleached all-purpose (plain) flour

1 cup (227 g) ground almonds, or 8 ounces (227 g) almond paste

2 egg whites, lightly beaten

8 ounces (113 g) pine nuts

Preheat the oven to 300°F (150°C/gas 2).

Lightly grease two large baking sheets. In a large bowl, sift the granulated and confectioners' sugar with the flour and set aside. In a medium bowl, mix the ground almonds or almond paste with the egg whites using a wooden spoon. If you are using almond paste, you may need an egg beater to break it up. When the almond–egg white mixture is smooth, add it to the flour-sugar mixture. Mix until well blended.

Drop mixture by rounded teaspoons 2¼ inches (5.5 cm) apart on the baking sheets. You should have rounds 1½ inches (4 cm) in diameter. Add 1 teaspoon (or more) of pine nuts to the top of each cookie and lightly press them into the dough. Bake 20 to 25 minutes, until golden. Place on a wire rack to cool. Sprinkle with confectioners' sugar.

98
Ricotta Pie/Grain Pie
Torta di Ricotta/Pasta di Grano

There are many variations of this classic. Included here are two of them: first the basic cheese pie, then an Eastertime variation of it. For the liqueur, you may use brandy, rum, or the Sicilian liqueur amaro. Orange slices soaked in the liqueur of your choice make an excellent topping for ricotta pies.

For a Sicilian, it would not be Easter without *pasta di grano*. This chewy, high-fiber modification of the ricotta torte has the cheese mixed with cooked whole wheat grain and baked in a round pie crust with a lattice top. The wheat berries take a while to cook, and the conscientious cook starts soaking them on Good Friday. Parboiled wheat berries are also available in many Italian stores, especially around Easter. You can usually find whole wheat grain in health food and specialty stores. Either use your own favorite crust or the crust suggested below, or buy packaged ready-made crust. If doing the latter, make sure you have extra to cut up for the lattice top. Also, since packaged crusts are not as deep as regular 9-inch (23 cm) pie plates, the filling made by the amounts given will probably make two pies with ready-made crusts.

Serves 8

Filling

1½ pounds (681 g) ricotta

1 cup (227 g) granulated sugar

5 eggs

1 tablespoon grated lemon zest

1 tablespoon grated orange zest

1 teaspoon cinnamon

1 teaspoon (5 mL) pure vanilla extract

2 tablespoons (30 mL) liqueur

2 tablespoons (28 g) semisweet chocolate chips

2 tablespoons (28 g) candied citron (optional)

Confectioners' (icing) sugar for dusting

Orange slices for serving

Preheat the oven to 325°F (160°C/gas 3).

Blend the ricotta cheese and granulated sugar in a bowl. In a separate bowl, beat the eggs, then fold them into the cheese mixture. Add the lemon and orange zest, cinnamon, vanilla, liqueur, chocolate chips, and candied citron.

Grease an 8-inch (20 cm)-square, 2-inch (5 cm)-deep baking dish or its equivalent. Pour cheese and egg mixture into a suitable buttered baking dish and bake for 1½ to 2 hours, until the top is brown and a toothpick inserted in the center comes out clean.

Allow torte to stand for at least 1 hour after it comes out of the oven. Sprinkle with confectioners' sugar and serve cold or at room temperature with fresh orange slices.

Variation: Grain Pie

½ cup (85 g) whole wheat berries
2 cups (473 mL) water
Ricotta Pie Filling (see above)

Crust
4 tablespoons (57 g) butter, softened
1 cup (784 g) unbleached all-purpose (plain) flour
¼ cup (57 g) almond meal
Iced water

Confectioners' (icing) sugar for dusting

Boil the whole wheat berries in the water, covered, for about 2 hours or until they are cooked and chewy. If the water boils away, add more. (Soaking them overnight will reduce boiling time.) Drain, reserving any extra water for soup stock if you like, and allow to cool.

Preheat the oven to 325°F (160°C/gas 3).

Prepare the filling as for the Ricotta Pie (see above). When you blend the ricotta and sugar in a bowl, fold in the cooked, cooled wheat berries. Add the other ingredients and prepare the crust.

To make the crust, cut the butter into the flour and almond meal with two forks or a pastry blender. When it looks like little peas, add iced water by the tablespoon and mix until you form a stiff dough. Separate into two balls, one about twice the size of the other. Roll out the large ball and place in the bottom of a 9-inch (23 cm) pie plate. Add the filling. (Do not overfill; if you have extra filling, bake it separately.) Roll out the remaining crust, cut it into 6 thin strips, and arrange them in a sunburst pattern on top of the filling, intersecting at the center of the pie's top and extending to the edges. Pinch the top ends to the sides of the crust. Bake for about 1½ to 2 hours, until top is brown and the center is dry when tested with a toothpick. Dust top with confectioners' sugar.

99
Cannoli

The most famous Sicilian sweet is cannoli, deep-fried pastries stuffed with sweetened ricotta. Originally the pastry was fried around bamboo cane, and that is where the name comes from. The hardest part about making cannoli is getting forms to fry the pastry on. Bamboo of 1-inch (2.5 cm) thickness is not that easy to come by. My family recipe starts, "Select an unpainted broom handle, four feet long or longer, and one inch in diameter, scrub it well, saw it into six-inch (15 cm) lengths, and sand the rough edges. . . . " There are metal forms available in Italian stores or in gourmet cookware shops. If you cannot find them, a hardwood dowel prepared as above will do. Make sure that the wood has not been treated in any way.

Cannoli must be filled right before serving or the cheese filling will make the pastry soggy. The shells can be left uncovered in a dry place, or the refrigerator, for up to a day or two before filling. The stuffing must sit for a few hours in the refrigerator to chill. It will keep for several days. You can prepare the shells and the filling ahead of time, and put them together while you are making after-dinner coffee.

Makes 8 cannoli

Shells

1¼ cups (230 g) unbleached all-purpose (plain) flour

1 teaspoon granulated sugar

¼ teaspoon cinnamon

Pinch of salt

1 egg, beaten

1 tablespoon (14 g) butter, melted

¼ cup (59 mL) white wine

Light vegetable oil for frying, to come to about 2 inches (5 cm) deep in the pot

Confectioners' (icing) sugar for dusting

Filling

1½ pounds (681 g) ricotta

1 cup (120 g) sifted confectioners' sugar

1 teaspoon (5 mL) pure vanilla extract

1 tablespoon (15 mL) liqueur (either orange liqueur such as Grand Marnier or Sicilian amaro)

1 tablespoon (14 g) finely chopped candied citron (optional)

¼ cup (57 g) semisweet chocolate chips

½ cup (92 g) shelled walnuts

Sift together the flour, granulated sugar, cinnamon, and salt onto a large platter, bread board, or countertop. Make a well in the dry ingredients and fold in three fourths of the beaten egg and the butter. Add the wine slowly, mixing as you do. The dough should be soft, smooth, and elastic. If the dough seems moist and sticky, add flour. If too dry, add more wine. Knead briefly. Place the dough in a floured bowl and let sit for 20 minutes.

On a floured board, roll the dough out thin, about ⅛ inch (.3 cm). Using a cookie cutter or suitable jar lid cut the dough into 4-inch (10 cm) circles. Roll each circle into a slightly oval shape, then wrap around the wooden or metal forms. Press the top edges together to hold them, then seal with a finger dipped in the remaining beaten egg.

Heat the oil until it is very hot but not smoking. Place as many of the dough-covered forms into the oil as will comfortably fit. The shells cook fast and swell in size, so do not overload the pan. Two or three at a time will be the limit of most pans. When the shells are brown on all sides, about 1 or 2 minutes, remove from the oil using a slotted metal spoon or metal tongs. Drain on brown paper or paper towels, and allow to cool. When cool enough to handle, remove the pastries from the forms by holding the pastry still while you gently twist the form. Dust pastries inside and out with sifted confectioners' sugar.

To make the filling, place the ricotta and sugar in a large bowl and mix gently with a wooden spoon. Add the vanilla, liqueur, and citron and stir further until all ingredients are well mixed. Put chocolate chips and walnuts in a blender or food processor and blend together briefly until the mixture is gritty. Stir half of this mixture into the filling and save the rest.

Place the filling in the refrigerator so it will chill thoroughly. Ten minutes before you are ready to fill the cannoli, place the filling in the freezer so it will thicken. Make sure it does not freeze at all! Fill the shells with a butter knife or small spoon, first one end, then the other. Sprinkle more sifted confectioners' sugar on the shells, and use the remaining nut and chocolate mixture to top off the ends.

John Penza, coauthor of *SICILIAN AMERICAN PASTA: 99 RECI-PES YOU CAN'T REFUSE*, is currently living in Eastern Long Island. Under the name John Okas, he has authored two novels—*ROUTES* and *THE FREEWAYFARERS' BOOK OF THE DEAD*, and is currently working on a third.

Miriam (Molly) **Dougenis,** a critically acclaimed artist, has exhib-ited in museums and galleries on Long Island, in New York City, and nationwide. Her work has been described as "achieving a lyri-cal intensity frequently absent in still-life subject matter . . . her colors are bold, her patterns original, and her sense of balance and form highly accomplished." She illustrated *SICILIAN AMERICAN PASTA*.